Count Rumford

It perhaps is appropriate that his own cloak-and-dagger activity should have inspired Sanborn C. Brown to begin collecting material for this biography of Benjamin Thompson, Count Rumford, who left his mark, as you will see, in the annals of espionage as well as on the records of physics. In his college days the author, who now is Associate Professor of Physics at the Massachusetts Institute of Technology, found Rumford interesting as a scientist, but it was not until World War II that he found Rumford fascinating as a man. While being trained in the methods of espionage and counterespionage in the Second World War, Professor Brown had occasion to read up on Rumford's scientific techniques in the use of secret inks and codes, and the more he read the more he wanted to know. The result of this enthusiasm has been a large body of scholarly research on Rumford's life, the publication of technical papers concerning Rumford's work, and the gathering of an unequaled collection of Rumford's apparatus and inventions.

Professor Brown was born on January 19, 1913, in Beirut, Lebanon, where his father, a physicist and astronomer, was teaching. From boyhood he expected to follow in the professional footsteps of his father, but he also had a strong leaning toward historical research. Geography and frail health combined to gratify his passion for history. Out of school for a year or so around the age of ten, he attached himself as mascot to a British archeological expedition studying cave dwellings in the Lebanon Mountains. Later he spent summers discovering and exploring Baal altars and Roman and Crusader castles, and, with the help of his father and brothers, made a plane-table survey of Roman watchtowers on the caravan routes to Damascus. He also discovered and mapped the boundaries of the Roman Emperor Hadrian's forest in the Lebanon Mountains.

Professor Brown came to the United States to attend Dartmouth College, where he received a B.A. in 1935 and an M.A. in 1937. (He has a Ph.D. from M.I.T., 1944.) In college an interest in old documents supplanted his hobby of archeology, and he soon found himself "chasing early physicists instead of Romans and Crusaders." In time Rumford became the focus of the new interest, and Professor Brown is engaged on a definitive biography, of which this small book might be called the overture.

His other writings include a textbook, *Basic Data of Plasma Physics* (Technology Press and John Wiley & Sons, New York, 1959); a book of conference proceedings, *International Education in Physics* (Technology Press and John Wiley & Sons, 1960); eighty technical papers on plasma physics, fourteen on science history, and seven on physics education.

He is a Fellow of the American Physical Society (Chairman, Division of Electron Physics, 1951–52); a Fellow of the American Association for Advancement of Science; a member of the American Association of Physics Teachers (Treasurer, 1955–62; Chairman, Committee on Apparatus for Educational Institutions, 1955–60; member of the Commission on College Physics); a Fellow of the American Academy of Arts and Sciences (Chairman, Rumford

Committee, 1955–58; Chairman, Committee on Educational Activities, 1957–61); a member of the History of Science Society and of the National Science Teachers Association; Technical Adviser to the United States Delegation to the Second United Nations International Conference on the Peaceful Uses of Atomic Energy, Geneva, 1958; Chairman of the Planning Committee, International Conference on Physics Education, Paris, 1960; National Lecturer, Society of the Sigma Xi, 1961; U.S. Delegate to the International Atomic Energy Agency Conference on Plasma Physics and Controlled Thermonuclear Fusion, Salzburg, 1961; member of the School Committee (Chairman, 1961–   ), Lexington, Massachusetts; International Union of Pure and Applied Physics (member of the U.S.A. National Committee; President of the International Commission on Physics Education); recipient of the Distinguished Service Citation awarded by the American Association of Physics Teachers, 1962.

COUNT RUMFORD

PHYSICIST EXTRAORDINARY

by Sanborn C. Brown

Published by Anchor Books
Doubleday & Company, Inc.
Garden City, New York
1962

Library of Congress Catalog Card Number 62–14130
Copyright © 1962 by Educational Services Incorporated
All Rights Reserved
Printed in the United States of America
First Edition

The Science Study Series

The Science Study Series offers to students and to the general public the writing of distinguished authors on the most stirring and fundamental topics of science, from the smallest known particles to the whole universe. Some of the books tell of the role of science in the world of man, his technology and civilization. Others are biographical in nature, telling the fascinating stories of the great discoverers and their discoveries. All the authors have been selected both for expertness in the fields they discuss and for ability to communicate their special knowledge and their own views in an interesting way. The primary purpose of these books is to provide a survey within the grasp of the young student or the layman. Many of the books, it is hoped, will encourage the reader to make his own investigations of natural phenomena.

The Series, which now offers topics in all the sciences and their applications, had its beginning in a project to revise the secondary schools' physics curriculum. At the Massachusetts Institute of Technology during 1956 a group of physicists, high school teachers, journalists, apparatus designers, film producers, and other specialists organized the Physical Science Study Committee, now operating as a part of Educational Services Incorporated, Watertown,

Massachusetts. They pooled their knowledge and experience toward the design and creation of aids to the learning of physics. Initially their effort was supported by the National Science Foundation, which has continued to aid the program. The Ford Foundation, the Fund for the Advancement of Education, and the Alfred P. Sloan Foundation have also given support. The Committee has created a textbook, an extensive film series, a laboratory guide, especially designed apparatus, and a teacher's source book.

The Series is guided by a Board of Editors, consisting of Bruce F. Kingsbury, Managing Editor; John H. Durston, General Editor; Paul F. Brandwein, the Conservation Foundation and Harcourt, Brace & World, Inc.; Francis L. Friedman, Massachusetts Institute of Technology; Samuel A. Goudsmit, Brookhaven National Laboratory; Philippe LeCorbeiller, Harvard University, and Gerard Piel, *Scientific American.*

Preface

It has been a source of real enjoyment to me to interrupt work on a comprehensive biography of Count Rumford to write this small volume for high school pupils and others interested in science. The stereotyped concept of a physicist is so drab and uninteresting that it becomes increasingly important to convince our young people that scientists can have lives as exciting as any. Although Rumford's life was more spectacular than most, the fact that he was a scientist, rather than in any way inhibiting his career, added to the excitement. Obviously, any volume as small as the present one must omit many details, incidents, and facts of a man's life, but I have tried to incorporate those particular elements which are of most interest for a volume written as background material for a first course in physics or as a layman's introduction to science.

In my search for historical material on Count Rumford, I am deeply indebted to a host of people for their continuing help over many years. In particular, I must acknowledge the help of two grants-in-aid from the Penrose Fund of the American Philosophical Society, given to me to collect photostatic copies of all existing manuscript material touching on the life and work of Benjamin Thompson. Many of the models of Rumford's scientific apparatus were built under my direction with money provided from the Rumford Fund of the American Academy of Arts and Sciences.

I owe special thanks to my two young editors, Stan Brown and Lee Macey, who spent many hours with both patience and enthusiasm giving me the critical comments of an age group for which I had not tried to write before. The red pencil wielded by my wife, Lois Brown, resulted in many improvements. Every author needs a good secretary and typist. The circumstances under which this book was written make my appreciation of Mrs. Shirley Orsula particularly heartfelt.

Sanborn C. Brown

Lexington, Massachusetts
November 1961

Contents

THE SCIENCE STUDY SERIES   ix

PREFACE   xi

1. COLONIAL BOYHOOD   1
   Apprenticeship. First Experiments.

2. COUNTRY GENTLEMAN OF CONCORD, N.H.   9
   An Auspicious Marriage. Major Thompson's
   Duties.

3. TORY SPY   17
   Invisible Ink. Thompson Flees the Country.

4. A COMFORTABLE LIFE IN LONDON . . .   23
   Thompson Resumes His Scientific Research.
   A Cruise with Admiral Hardy's Fleet. The
   Practical Side of Physics. The LaMotte Spy
   Case.

5. OFFICER OF THE DRAGOONS   33
   The Economics of Raising a Regiment. Two
   Skirmishes.

6. A SOLDIER OF FORTUNE IN BAVARIA . . .   37
   Two Influential Contacts. Sir Benjamin.
   Bavarian Colonel.

7. COURT LIFE AND RESEARCH   47

Thermal Conductivity of Cloth. Thompson's Discovery of Convection Currents.

8. THOMPSON AS A SOCIAL REFORMER . . .   55

A Scheme to Put Beggars to Work. Life in the Workhouse.

9. A SCIENTIFIC APPROACH TO NUTRITION . .   63

Maximum Nutrition at Minimum Cost. How to Make a "Rumford Soup."

10. THE VERSATILE INVENTOR   69

Munich's English Garden. The Economics of the Kitchen. Measuring the Intensity of Light: Rumford's Photometer. Improved Lamps.

11. SIR BENJAMIN BECOMES COUNT RUMFORD   83

A Spectacular Rise to Power. Count of the Holy Roman Empire.

12. CONTRIBUTIONS TO THE THEORY OF HEAT   89

The Caloric Theory. The Cannon-Boring Experiments. Significance of Rumford's Contributions. Further Experiments Designed to Disprove the Caloric Theory. Freezing and Contraction of Water.

13. SUCCESS IN ENGLAND AND BAVARIA . . .   107

Essay on the Improvement of Fireplaces. The Rumford Prizes. A Military "Battle" and Promotion to General. Invention of a Portable Field Stove.

14. RUMFORD'S ATTEMPT TO RETURN TO
    AMERICA   121

    Proposal to Establish a U.S. Military
    Academy. Rumford Declines.

15. THE ROYAL INSTITUTION OF GREAT BRITAIN   127

    Public Support of Rumford's Plan. The
    Arrival of Young Humphry Davy. James
    Watt Protests. Return to the Continent.

16. THE COURTSHIP OF MADAME LAVOISIER . .   141

17. DISHARMONY: LEGAL AND MARITAL . . .   145

    Rumford Designs a Lamp. Involved in a
    Lawsuit. Marital Discord.

18. PRACTICAL SCIENCE   153

    Lighting Improvements. Steam Heat.

19. LAST WORKS   159

    A Drip Coffeepot. Cuvier's Eulogy.

CONCLUSION   165

APPENDIX   167

BIBLIOGRAPHY   169

INDEX   173

Count Rumford

CHAPTER 1

Colonial Boyhood

The interest of the scientifically inclined youth of any era reflects the technological interest of the scientific community in which they live. Thus we can tell a good deal about the puzzling questions of physics in the mid-eighteenth century when we discover a teen-ager of that time making the following requests: "Please to give the Nature, Essence, Begining of Existance, and Rise of the Wind in General—with the whole Theory thereof, so as to be Able to Answer all Questions relative thereto." "Please to Give the Direction of the Rays of Light from a Luminous Body, to an Opake, and the Reflection frome the Opake Body to Another Equally Dence & Opake vizt. the Direction of the rays of the Luminous Body to that of ye opake, and the Direction to the other opake Body." "Please to inform me in what manner fire operates upon Clay, to Change the Colour from the Natural Colour to red and from red to Black &c and how it operates upon Silver to Change it to Blue."

These words were written in August 1769, by a scientifically talented boy, Benjamin Thompson, whose contributions to physics were very real throughout his life and yet whose name is almost unknown today. As we shall see, his research in pure physics was remarkably ingenious, and his practical improvements had a great effect on the society of his day. Unfortunately, his personality had many defects. He lacked moral principles, and his short-comings alienated people from considering him a great scientific leader. Thompson's fame has been dimmed in an obscurity that would not have existed if he had been judged on the basis of his scientific contributions alone. As a physicist he was brilliant.

Benjamin Thompson was born on March 26, 1753, to a simple farm family in Woburn, Massachusetts. His father died when he was very young. His mother remarried and reared a large family. When Benjamin was thirteen years old, his family indentured him to a tradesman so that he could help to earn his own living and supplement the family's meager resources. First he went to work for Mr. John Appleton, who was an importer of dry-goods merchandise in the seaport town of Salem, about twenty miles from home. Benjamin had been working there for three years when, in 1769, the merchants of New England decided to protest the high taxes the British government levied upon them. They banded together and signed a non-importation agreement. The resulting loss in business so harassed the signers of this agreement that Mr. Appleton could not support even his youthful clerk from Woburn, and Benjamin lost his job. It was in the interval before he had found another job that he wrote the three questions about the wind, light, and color, which we have just seen.

Apprenticeship

On October 11, 1769, a Mr. Hopestill Capen wrote to John Appleton asking him about "a young

Ladd, not long since that lived with you, named Benj^a Thompson" and inquiring about "his True Character as to his Honesty, Temper and Qualifications as a Shop Keeper." Soon thereafter, Benjamin Thompson went to work for Mr. Capen in a dry-goods shop in a building that still stands near Fanueil Hall, in Boston. Although the family finances surely benefited, being stuck behind a counter to sell cloth and notions was hardly the life for an imaginative young man, particularly at a time when the ferment of revolution was bubbling.

We know a remarkable amount about Benjamin's life in these days because he kept a diary in which he recorded as varied a selection of entries as you might expect from any active boy of seventeen. It is clear from the pages of his diary that he was particularly interested in the manufacture of gunpowder, rockets, and firecrackers. Benjamin lost his job, and one story has it that he almost blew himself up trying to make a skyrocket display in honor of the repeal of the Stamp Act. The explosion was more than Mr. Capen could bear, and he fired the young clerk. One feels sure that while Benjamin worked for Mr. Capen he was searching for other occupations that would be more fun and would stimulate his intellectual curiosity. Benjamin had been in Boston less than a year when the local physician of Woburn, Dr. Hay, agreed to take him on as an apprentice. We know that Hopestill Capen was not undone by this decision, since he wrote to Benjamin's mother that he "oftener found her son *under* the counter with gimlets, knife and saw constructing some little machine or looking over some book of science, than *behind* it arranging the cloths or waiting upon customers."

First Experiments

The apprenticeship with Dr. Hay did not continue long enough to turn Benjamin's attention seriously to medicine, but it did stamp him as being interested in intellectual pursuits and also gave him more time to pursue his scientific education. During colonial times very few pupils attended school beyond what we now think of as the elementary grades, and most boys interested in science or engineering picked up what education they could from their elders and friends. Benjamin Thompson's education was typical. One of his friends, a somewhat older boy named Loammi Baldwin, was very influential in guiding him in the field which then was called natural philosophy and which now we call physics. He and Loammi organized a "scientific society," and the two boys exchanged problems and puzzles for a number of years. We know of various experimental projects that Thompson undertook. He is supposed to have tried hard to construct a perpetual-motion machine, and we have a fairly clear idea from the accounts in his diary of his construction of an electrical machine similar in principle to the Van de Graaff generator of today. It is startling to compare the amount of labor involved in Benjamin's undertaking with the time that many modern high school boys spend on their science fair projects. Entries in his diary include "An Acc^t of what Work I have Done towardes Getting an Electrical Machine—Two or 3 days work Mak^g Wheele, ½ day work Mak^g pattern for small Conductor, mak^g pattern for Electrometer, ½ day and a horse from hence to B. Tays then to W. Youngs, from thence to Ich^a. Richardsons to try to get Ma-

chine Made, 4 Journeys Down to Ich\ª. Richardsons Shop. 3 Journeys to Cowdreys. 1 Journey to
Boston, Aug\ᵗ 16\ᵗʰ as I think."

In the days when formal schooling was uncommon, it was up to the individual to cultivate his own
self-discipline to protect his attention to studies from
the competition of the more exciting interruptions
of teen-age life. The distractions were made particularly vital in the early seventeen-seventies by
the realities of revolutionary politics. Benjamin
Thompson was surely tempted by these more exciting possibilities, but he made himself a rigid sched-
ule and recorded it in detail in his diary, perhaps
to make it seem more official to himself. His sched-
ule was:

> Munday—Anatomy
> Tewsday—Anatomy
> Wednesday—Institutes of Physic
> Thursday—Surgery
> Fryday—Chimistry with the Materia Medica
> Saturday—Physick ½ and Surgery ½

Each hour of the day was also planned in advance.

> 1
> 2
> 3   Sleep.
> 4
> 5
> 6   Get up at Six oclock and wash my hands and
> 7   face.
> 8   From 6 to 8, Exercise ½ and Study ½
> 9
> 10 From 8 till 10 Breakfast Attend prayers etc.
> 11
> 12 From 10 to 12 Study all the time.
> 1
> 2

3   From 1 to 4 Study—Constantly.
4   From 4 to 5 Relieve my mind by some
5   Diversion or Excersise.
6   From 5 till Bed time follow what my inclina-
7   tion Leads me to whether it be to a broad or
8   stay at home and read either Anatomy, Phys-
9   ics, or Chymistry or any other book I want to
10 Peruse.
11
12 Sleep.

During his apprenticeship with Dr. Hay, he submitted his first scientific paper for publication. It
was a detailed and rather grotesque drawing of an
abnormal child, born in Woburn on April 16, 1771.
Although this paper was submitted to the American Philosophical Society, in Philadelphia, and duly
recorded as having been received, it never was
published. We know of the details of the drawing
because he copied it in his diary. We also see in
his diary that he did a good many things other than
pay strict attention to Dr. Hay's office in Woburn.
He recorded that he attended some of Professor
Winthrop's lectures in natural philosophy at Harvard, a statement partly responsible for the legend
that he went to Harvard, although there is no record of him at that institution. He also taught country school for a few weeks at a time in neighboring
towns and carried on lively experiments with his
friend Loammi Baldwin, some of which were more
spectacular than sensible.

One experiment, which must have brought the
boys as near to committing suicide as is possible,
was an attempted repetition of the famous kite experiment of Benjamin Franklin. This was described
by Loammi Baldwin as follows:

In July 1771, I constructed an electrical kite, the stem of which was about four and a half feet long and the breadth at the extremities of the bow about two feet. . . . A very small wire was placed along the stem . . . and communicated with the main flying line by which the kite was raised. This line was a small hard cord and was soaked in water previous to raising the kite. My design was to make some experiments in the time of a thunder-shower. . . . A few days later there appeared a very handsome thundershower . . . attended with the most piercing shafts of lightning and tremen-dous thunder that I had ever beheld or heard. . . . I adjusted the lines of the kite . . . and raised it to the height of some lofty trees which stood near my house. By this time I discovered a rare medium of fire between my eyes and the kite—I cast my eyes toward the ground—the same appear-ance was there—I turned myself around—and the same appearance still between me and every object which I cast my eyes upon—I felt myself somewhat alarmed at the appearance. . . . All this time the fiery atmosphere was increasing and extending it-self with some faint gentle flashing, but with no other effect upon me than a general weakness of my joints and limbs and a kind of listless feeling. . . . However, it was sufficient to discourage me from any further attempts at that time. I drew in the kite and retired. . . . I went into my house where I found my parents and family vastly more surprised than I had been myself, who informed me that I appeared to them to be in the midst of a large bright flame of fire attended with flashing, and expected every moment to see me fall a sacri-fice to the flame.

Another experiment must have given Dr. Hay considerable pause to wonder whether his youthful apprentice was seriously interested in medicine or might be just dabbling in science for fun. The physician told of coming home one day to hear a pig squealing on the second floor of his house. Rushing upstairs, he found that young Benjamin had operated on a pig to remove the windpipe, and was busily blowing through the pig's bronchial tubes to produce the spectacular effect that so alarmed the good doctor.

Whether it was Benjamin himself, his parents, or Dr. Hay who made the final decision we will never know, but Benjamin Thompson was relieved of his duties as apprentice to Dr. Hay early in 1772.

One of the standard procedures for a young man to follow in search of an education in colonial America was teaching younger children. And Benjamin Thompson's board at the home of Dr. Hay had been interrupted on two occasions while he was "keeping school." During the winter of 1771 he taught school at Wilmington, Massachusetts, and during the spring of 1772 he was doing the same thing at Bradford, Massachusetts. On leaving Dr. Hay, he tried his hand at teaching as a profession.

CHAPTER 2

Country Gentleman of Concord, N.H.

The school system in colonial days was very different from what we are used to today. Reading, writing, and arithmetic were the essentials, and a schoolmaster needed to know only the rudiments of these three subjects to be equipped to teach. Leading citizens of a town would get together and find a suitable young man to instruct their children. Often the teaching took place in someone's home. It was under this kind of system that Benjamin Thompson was invited to go to Concord, New Hampshire. The most influential man in town was the Reverend Timothy Walker, an aging clergyman who had led the people of Concord through desperate struggle against the rigors of an unsettled North, hostile Indians, and even a grim plague of rattlesnakes. The Walker family originally came from Woburn, and it was therefore not unusual that they had heard of the bright lad Benjamin Thompson.

An Auspicious Marriage

For many years the town of Concord had been dominated by two men, the Reverend Mr. Walker and Benjamin Rolfe, a wealthy landed proprietor of that part of New Hampshire. Besides being a great friend of Walker and the richest man in the countryside, Rolfe had held about every political office in the town and was a colonel in the New Hampshire Militia. He was also a friend and confidant of the Royal Governor of New Hampshire. A year before Colonel Rolfe died, at the age of sixty, he married Timothy Walker's daughter, who was thirty years younger. When Benjamin Thompson arrived in Concord, she had been a widow for only a few months. Sarah Walker's husband had left her a wealthy woman, and at her age she must have longed for the gay life that her social position would have allowed her in the fashionable circles of Portsmouth, New Hampshire. Thus, when the handsome schoolmaster of nineteen, almost six feet tall, with carefully powdered auburn hair, arrived in town under the auspices of her family, she found him attractive in many ways. In 1772, less than four months after they met, the schoolteacher and the widow eleven years his senior were married. When teased in later years about his rapid rise to fortune, Benjamin Thompson denied all thought of scheming. "She married me," he said, "not I her." Whoever did the actual proposing is not important. Benjamin did not have to be a schoolmaster any longer; he settled down to manage his wife's estate and to make himself useful to the Royal Governor, John Wentworth.

Throughout his life Benjamin Thompson used his interest and ability in science and technology as a technique for calling attention to himself, particularly in those circles where favors and prestige might be found. This method was most effective with Governor Wentworth. Thompson proposed a scientific expedition, a White Mountains survey, which he outlined in a letter to one of his former teachers, the Reverend Samuel Williams, under whose influence he had come a couple of years earlier when he was teaching school in Bradford. "He [Governor Wentworth] said it would be extremely agreeable, seemed excessively pleased with the plan, promised to do all that lay in his power to forward it—said that he had a number of mathematical instruments (such as two or three telescopes, barometers, thermometer, compass, etc.) at Wentworth House (at Wolfeboro, only about thirty miles from the mountains) all which, together with his library, should be at our service. That he should be extremely glad to wait on us, and to crown all, he promised if there were no public business which rendered his presence in Portsmouth absolutely necessary that he would take his tent equipage and go with us to the mountains and tarry with us and assist us till our survey, which he said he supposed would take about twelve or fourteen days!!!—!!—!!!!! [sic]."

Although in his younger days in Woburn Thompson had been very scornful of the farmer's life, in Concord we find him turning his attention enthusiastically to agriculture. When we look for reasons for this change of heart, we find them in the fact that Governor Wentworth was an ardent experimenter with agricultural products, and was spending large sums on his estate in Wolfeboro, New Hampshire, on this hobby. Thompson himself wrote to Loammi Baldwin, "As I am engaged in husbandry, I have a mind to try some experiments in that way, and as my mother informs me you are about to send to England for some garden seeds against the spring, I should be extremely obliged if you would send the enclosed memorandum to London so that I may have the seeds mentioned therein as early in the spring as possible. I have eighteen or twenty acres of land to lay down to grass in ye spring, and shall want the grass seed very much and very early." Starting with "a hundred pounds best bed clover seed," his long lists include three different kinds of clover, three varieties of grass, five kinds of cabbage, four of turnip, six kinds of pea, five of oat and barley, and fifteen varieties of wheat.

The outward signs of the favor with which Governor Wentworth looked upon this brilliant young colonial squire were spectacular. Within six months of the time that Benjamin Thompson had married into fortune and leisure, Governor Wentworth presented to this twenty-year-old boy a major's commission in the New Hampshire Militia. People's feelings got hurt as easily in 1773 as they do today, and the professional soldiers of the New Hampshire regiments were furious.

With a blithe disregard of the bitterness over his appointment, Benjamin Thompson set to work to recruit officers and men from all the neighboring towns for his Fifteenth Regiment of Militia. His records of the towns he visited and the people he solicited, and even the details of the uniforms that his regiment were to wear, give us a very clear picture of his labors in this regard. As he wrote to Loammi Baldwin, "I have been extremely busy this summer or I should have given myself the pleasure of coming to see you, but have not been able to get away as yet." He could not have been totally engrossed in his regimental duties, however, for in the same letter he proposed to Baldwin a problem on quite a different subject: "A certain cistern has three brass cocks, one of which will empty it in fifteen minutes, one in thirty minutes, and the

other in sixty minutes. Query: How long would it
take to empty the cistern if all three of the cocks
were opened at once?"*

Major Thompson's Duties

Why should a man as skilled in public administration as was Governor Wentworth appoint young
Thompson to such a rank when it obviously would
embitter the professional soldiers in the New Hampshire Army, and when the injury would be made
particularly painful by Thompson's public display
of his military position? Governor Wentworth's behavior was neither fickle nor hasty but a move
which demonstrated his shrewdness and a clear insight into the personality of his protégé. Revolution
was in the air, but the farmers of New Hampshire,
while many of them had fought against the Indians,
knew nothing of military tactics employed by
the Continental Armies. The colonists desperately
needed drillmasters and military instructors, and
were willing to pay tremendous bonuses to entice
British Regulars into deserting to the armies that
were being assembled secretly throughout the colonies. To combat this subversion, the Royal Gover-
nors did all they could to enlist spies and informers
for the royal cause.

Everything about Benjamin Thompson told the
Governor that this young man had everything to
gain and nothing to lose by making himself useful
and available to the Tories. He was overbearingly
ambitious and evidently willing to plunge into marriage for money. Furthermore, he was in a particularly fortunate position to keep track of itinerant

* The answer is 8.57 minutes.

workmen who might be deserters from the British Army in disguise. He managed large farms and woodlands, and employed dozens of men to work his holdings. We know that not all the discussions between Thompson and Wentworth concerned surveys of the White Mountains or experiments with wheat and clover. The Governor and the Major made a deal profitable to both. Thompson agreed to become a full-fledged informer for the Governor in return for a social position that was almost unimaginable for a man so young. Governor Wentworth supplied him with a British soldier in disguise to do the actual checking on men in the vicinity who might be deserters from the British Army stationed in Boston.

At a time when the colonists were building up to open rebellion against the British Crown, anyone who seemed less than enthusiastic about the cause of "freedom" was suspected of treachery. Benjamin Thompson not only received favors from the Royal Governor but was very open about his feelings that true patriotism demanded adherence to the established forces of law and order. It is not to be wondered at that the citizens of Concord looked on him with considerable suspicion, mounting finally to open hostility. Early in December 1774, Major Thompson was summoned before the Committee of Safety to answer charges of being unfriendly to the cause of freedom. This semi-legal body was set up to examine the political attitudes of the local citizens, and it gave Mr. Thompson a full-scale trial. However, no proof of treachery was forthcoming, and the case was dismissed.

The hotheads of the countryside were by no means satisfied by the judgment of the Committee of Safety, with its reliance on provable facts. A week before Christmas, Major Thompson learned that the enthusiasts for the cause of liberty were gathering to march on the Thompson mansion to tar and feather him and ride him out of town on a rail. Major Thompson was not the sort of man to be caught in such a predicament. He borrowed his brother-in-law's best horse and galloped off into the night toward Boston, leaving his wife to look after their baby, Sarah, and his aged father-in-law to pacify the angry mob. He never went back.

CHAPTER 3

Tory Spy

It was not likely that Benjamin Thompson's political leanings would change because an enraged mob had driven him out of Concord. The incident which inflamed popular feeling against him was damning. A leading citizen of Concord had visited Boston and recognized one of Thompson's disguised soldiers in the uniform of one of General Gage's British regiments guarding the city. Since Thompson was already working so closely with the British, it was natural that he would flee to Boston and report his plight to General Gage's headquarters. Boston was the center of Tory activity. It was a fact that many honorable colonists were Tories.

General Gage, the highest British officer in the Massachusetts Bay Colony, was extremely eager to obtain as much information as he could about the build-up of anti-British sentiment, particularly in the vicinity of his headquarters. The records show that after Thompson fled from Concord to Boston, he returned to his home in Woburn and tried to offer his services as a New Hampshire Major to Colonel George Washington in Cambridge. News of his behavior in New Hampshire, however, preceded him, and he failed to obtain official standing in the Massachusetts Colonial Militia. Then he settled down in Woburn, to all outward appearances calmly waiting for something to happen. Although these appearances may have led people to believe Thompson was merely an idle gentleman, documents uncovered in the secret British records of the American Revolution show that he was an extremely well-informed and clever spy. The use he made of his knowledge of chemistry in compounding secret ink showed that he had learned his laboratory technique well.

Invisible Ink

The first actual fighting in the Revolution broke out in Lexington on April 19, 1775. Thereafter, anything that passed in and out of Boston was subject to scrutiny, both by the soldiers of the colonies and the soldiers of the crown. On May 6, 1775, an innocent-looking letter, reproduced in Fig. 1, passed

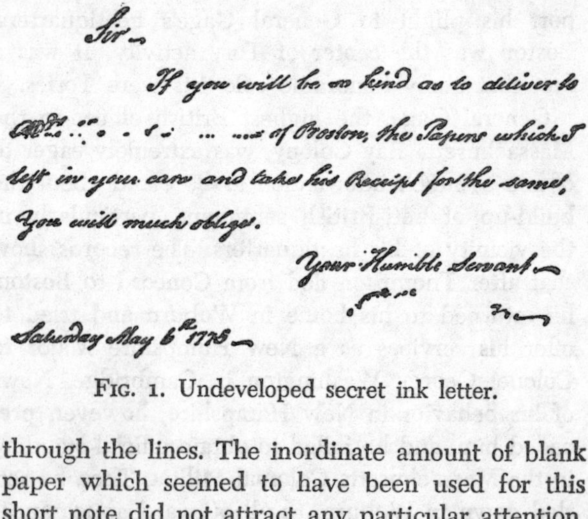
Sir—

If you will be so kind as to deliver to [illegible] of Boston, the Papers which I left in your care and take his Receipt for the same, You will much oblige.

Your Humble Servant—

Saturday May 6th 1775—

FIG. 1. Undeveloped secret ink letter.

through the lines. The inordinate amount of blank paper which seemed to have been used for this short note did not attract any particular attention, and the letter was duly delivered to somebody in Boston with whom Thompson had been in intimate contact and who, therefore, knew that this note contained an important intelligence written in secret ink.

There is no doubt that if the letter had been detected, Benjamin Thompson would have been hanged immediately, and yet this application of his scientific education was so good that he was willing to risk his life on the assumption that his treachery was undetectable. The secret ink that he used was gallo-tannic acid, which was obtained by soaking powdered nutgalls in water. Nutgalls, the round growths which are to be found all around Woburn in the woods on the leaves of oak trees, are a readily available source of the basic chemical. Writing on modern bleached paper with this kind of gallo-tannic acid would not be invisible because of its slightly yellowish tinge, but on the yellow handmade paper of the day it was completely invisible. This "infusion of nutgalls" had been described as early as 1480 by Jean Batista Porta as a secret ink, and since Porta's account was in the standard references of the day, there is little doubt that Thompson had come across a description. As a matter of fact, he undoubtedly learned while he was working for Dr. Hay in Woburn that nutgall powder was sold as a common anti-diarrhea drug. Indeed, about this time he wrote to a friend, "Since I left Boston I have enjoyed but a very indifferent share of health, having been much troubled by putrid bilious disorders."

This secret ink could be developed only by a special chemical, ferrous sulphate, as described by Porta. Thompson, therefore, must have made arrangements in Boston for his secret intelligence to be developed. In the quoted letter of May 6, he said he "came out of Boston a few days before the affair at Lexington on the 19th of April." We therefore have the evidence that he could have arranged for this proper chemical treatment to be given to his innocent cover letter, which was written in a black carbon ink. After proper treatment, the secret message appeared as is shown in Fig. 2.

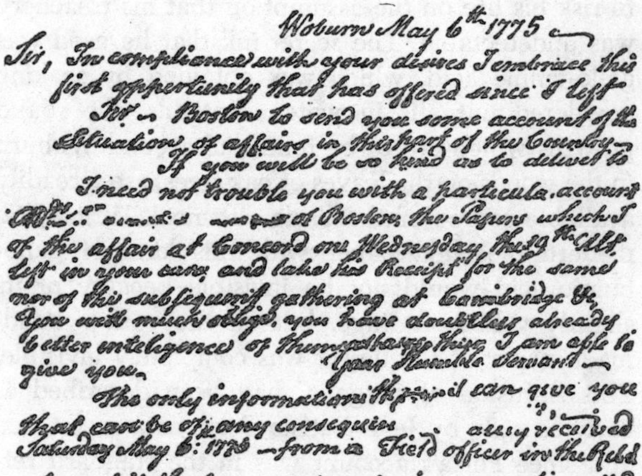

FIG. 2. First page of the developed secret ink letter.

Thompson Flees the Country

The outbreak of open hostilities against the British brought an influx of New Hampshire Militiamen to George Washington's army in Cambridge. It was not long before Thompson's open friendliness with the New Hampshire Governor became common knowledge around Woburn, and Thompson was called before another Committee of Safety, this time in Massachusetts. Again, nothing could be proved against him, and although he was released and allowed to go, he was never again to be really free of surveillance by his fellow-colonists.

The soldiers in Washington's army were ill-equipped and improperly fed, living under conditions that led to a serious outbreak of typhoid. Because the soldiers who were sick were sent home to recover, the epidemic spread quickly to many areas. Thompson himself came down with the disease in the middle of August and was unable to move about until early October. As soon as he was well, he made no secret of the fact that he was planning to flee, and in the middle of October 1775, he left his native Woburn and joined the British ranks in the city of Boston. He and his wife already had parted, never to meet again.

One of the most intimate glimpses we have of the details of the American Revolutionary Army before Boston in 1775 comes from a long memorandum entitled "Miscellaneous Observations Upon the State of the Rebel Army," which Benjamin Thompson wrote for the British High Command as soon as he went to Boston. His knowledge of the Greater Boston area must have been useful to the harassed British generals trying to hold on to the besieged city. By March 1776, however, the position of the British troops in Boston was untenable, and the city was abandoned. The British, with as many Tory sympathizers as could be accommodated, sailed for Halifax, Nova Scotia. The official dispatches of this reverse in the fortunes of the King's Army were entrusted to a Judge William Brown to take to London, and in Judge Brown's company sailed also the dashing young Loyalist from Massachusetts, Major Benjamin Thompson.

CHAPTER 4

A Comfortable Life in London

When Benjamin Thompson landed in London, in the early summer of 1776, he arrived not as a political refugee but as a self-assured expert on the details of the fighting in and around Boston. Since the previous November, the Secretary of State for the Colonies, under King George III, was Lord George Germain. Germain had spent a good part of his life as a professional soldier, but he had been court-martialed out of the British Army for cowardice in battle, and had turned to politics to bolster his damaged reputation. Since his administration was characterized by a determination to hold his job through pleasing the King, the news of the fall of Boston was a threat to his new career. Indeed, the public clamor that arose might well have swept him from his post had there not appeared at his elbow a brilliantly informed young man whose version of the affair in Massachusetts was so convincing that Germain was able to weather the storm without much difficulty. Thompson, never one to hide his light under a bushel, let it be understood that his position in Boston was rather more important than the facts would have warranted. Nevertheless, his keen powers of observation and his analytical turn of mind gave the Colonial Office more insight into the American Revolution than it usually had. Furthermore, Benjamin Thompson was not unknown to the British government. He had made an extremely foresighted deal with Governor Wentworth, of New Hampshire. If anyone wanted to question Thompson's credentials, he had only to point to such dispatches as that which Wentworth had sent in 1774 to the Earl of Dartmouth, Germain's predecessor: "I have been successful in prevailing on soldiers deserting from the King's troops at Boston to return to their duty through the spirited and prudent activity of Major Thompson, a Militia officer of New Hampshire, whose management, the General writes me, promises further success."

Of course, we do not know what Thompson told Lord George, but we do know that he so impressed the Secretary of State for the Colonies that almost immediately he was made Germain's private secretary, and for the next five years was to be found ever at Germain's elbow. As time went on, the activities of the American Revolution moved southward from Massachusetts, and Thompson's information was no longer important. Nevertheless, he lost no luster in the eyes of the government. We find that by 1779 his official position was that of Secretary of the Province of Georgia, a mark of royal favor, although the position was only nominal since the British had lost authority in that province. By September 1780, Thompson had obtained an office of significance, becoming Under Secretary of State for the Northern Department. In this position he wielded real power, for not only was he directly responsible for recruiting, equipping, and transporting the British forces, but he also was the primary contact between American Loyalists in London and the British government.

Thompson Resumes His Scientific Research

Thompson's official actions are chronicled in many volumes of the British Foreign Office files, but these are the rather dry and frustrating records of inefficient officialdom. Much more interesting to us is the story of his development at this time as a research physicist, and his attempts to use the results of pure science in his dealings with his fellowmen. Thompson went to London as a major in the Colonial Militia and was therefore considered primarily a military man. But as he rose higher in the English Court, he found new leisure, which he used in "philosophical" experimentation along military lines.

During the summer of 1778, Thompson started some studies in the force of fired gunpowder, performing his experiments at Stoneland Lodge, a country estate belonging to Lord George. As we have seen, Thompson was interested as a boy in the chemistry and physics of gunpowder, about whose basic science very little was known, although explosives were, of course, the primary material of the soldier. What causes the force produced by exploding gunpowder was a matter of deep concern to many scientists of the day, and Thompson turned his attention to a device which would allow the forces of gunpowders of different compositions to be measured in the laboratory. In 1742, Benjamin Robins, a noted mathematician and Engineer-General of the East India Company, had invented the ballistic pendulum for measuring the initial velocity of bullets shot from guns. Robins' ballistic pendulum was basically the same as the device still used in the physics laboratory for measuring the velocity of bullets. The pendulum operates on the principle of the conservation of momentum. A bullet is shot into a heavy wooden pendulum, and the distance the pendulum swings is measured. One can calculate the velocity of the bullet if its mass and the mass of the pendulum are known. Thompson's modification of Robins' experiment was to measure the recoil of the gun rather than the swing of the pendulum. He believed that because the bullets and cannon balls used in the muskets and cannons of the day fitted the bores of the weapons so loosely, much of the force of the gunpowder was lost in leakage around the missile, and thus the full strength of the explosion was not measured by the velocity of the missile itself. Thompson's own picture of his experimental setup is shown in Fig. 3.

Thompson's first published paper was "An Account of Some Experiments Upon Gunpowder," which appeared in the Philosophical Transactions of the Royal Society in 1781. This publication subjected him to a good deal of criticism because of his apparent claim to supposedly new ideas. Nevertheless, the paper attracted considerable attention and, later in the year, was mainly responsible for his being elected a Fellow of the Royal Society.

A Cruise with Admiral Hardy's Fleet

In retrospect Benjamin Thompson's scientific experiments seem always to have been woven in with his political schemes, and his experiments in Stoneland Lodge led directly to his connection with Admiral Hardy's fleet. Lord George arranged for Thompson to be attached as a guest to Admiral Hardy's fleet, which went on maneuvers off the

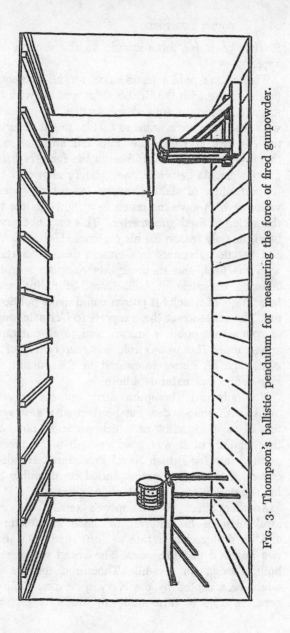

Fig. 3. Thompson's ballistic pendulum for measuring the force of fired gunpowder.

English coast for three months in the summer of 1779.

Thompson's public justification for his presence on the cruise with the British ships was his wish to arrange for large-scale and spectacular experiments with the fleet's heavy guns so that he might observe the distance at which the balls fell into the sea, thereby continuing his studies on the force of fired gunpowder. As he wrote, the gunnery allowed him "opportunities of making several interesting observations which gave me much new light relative to the action of fired gunpowder." This may not have been the only reason for his presence. He sent long and detailed accounts to Germain during his stay with the fleet, and these reports compose a truly amazing chronicle of inefficiency, stupidity, and ineptitude, of which his patron could make political use. The existence of these reports to Germain was, of course, not publicly known, and to all outward appearances Thompson's role was merely that of a gentleman of leisure interested in the pursuit of knowledge and natural philosophy.

Not only did Thompson carry out his experiments with gunpowder, but he devised a new system of naval signaling of which we know none of the details, but it was good enough to be incorporated into the British Naval Procedures. His discovery of this signal system added considerably to his reputation as a natural philosopher.

Another effect of Thompson's cruise was an awakening of his interest in naval architecture, and he designed a frigate of forty guns to carry two hundred and fifty men. The vessel was never built, though for a while Thompson thought it might be accepted by the Navy surveyors. Failing here, he tried to raise sufficient funds by private subscription for its construction, but his plan never matured.

We have an interesting contemporary view of Thompson, found in a diary of Judge Curwen. For thirty years previous to the outbreak of war, Samuel Curwen had been Deputy Judge of Admiralty and Provisional Impost Office in Salem, Massachusetts. A political refugee in London, he was destitute and felt himself to be entitled to financial help from a government he had served so long. "Went early in order to be at Mr. Benjamin Thompson's on time, and being a little before, heard he was not returning from Lord George Germain's where he always breakfasts, dines and sups, so great a favorite is he. . . . On second return, found him at his lodging. He received me in a friendly manner, taking me by the hand, talked with great freedom and promised to remember and serve me in the way I proposed him. Promises are easily made and genteel dilusive encouragement, the stable article of trade belonging to the courtier's profession. I put no hopes on the fair appearances of outward behavior, though it is uncandid to suppose all need to deceive. . . . This young man, when a shop lad to my next neighbor, ever appeared active, goodnatured and sensible, by a strange concurrence of events he is now Under Secretary to the American Secretary of State, Lord George Germain, a Secretary to Georgia, Inspector of all clothing sent to America, and Lieutenant Colonel Commandant of Horse Dragoons at New York. His income arising from these sources is, I have been told, near 7000 a year—a sum infinitely beyond his most sanguine expectations. He is, besides, a member of the Royal Society."

The Practical Side of Physics

In some ways, Thompson was very much of a nonconformist. The gulf between the natural philosophers, whom today we call pure physicists, and the artisans and inventors, which included those whom we now consider applied physicists and engineers, was very great. The natural philosophers considered the artisans crude and ill-educated, while the inventors scorned the natural philosophers as impractical dreamers. One of Benjamin Thompson's real contributions to the development of science was his realization that practical devices and improvements could stem directly from basic studies of pure physics. We see him turning his attention to the fundamental properties of nature, time and again, in ways that also were directly applicable to his everyday problems.

Typical of his searching for an understanding of nature as it applied to the common problems of life were Thompson's studies of the strength of silk. One of his major concerns in his official position as Under Secretary of the Northern Department was the clothing sent to the British soldiers fighting the American Revolution. The operation of the Army in the seventeen-eighties was very different from what we take for granted today. Quartermaster's corps did not exist. Thompson operated his department according to the custom of the day by buying the uniforms at his own expense in London and selling them to the Army in New York at the best price he could arrange. This highly speculative procedure could make one immensely wealthy, and it was therefore very much to his advantage to guarantee that the uniforms he shipped from London would be acceptable at the end of their arduous journey across the ocean. Anyone who has seen pictures of the soldiers' uniforms in colonial days must be impressed by the extravagant use of silk, particularly in the uniforms of the officers. Natural silk, especially when improperly cleaned and treated, is very susceptible to mildew and rot, and the long ocean voyage from London to America created a real hazard for the uniforms destined to adorn the parade grounds of the American scene. Thompson undertook a fundamental study of the tensile strength of silk fibers under all kinds of conditions, and although his political fortunes were to undergo such rapid changes that this work never came to any real conclusion, his attempted application of pure research to the practical problems of everyday administration was a pattern that characterized his conduct of affairs throughout his whole life.

The LaMotte Spy Case

One of London's most spectacular spy incidents in the American Revolution was the case of La-Motte. LaMotte was accused of being a spy for the French after a member of his organization, disgruntled at the size of his own cut, had turned state's evidence. The spy was caught red-handed with detailed plans of naval operations and maneuvers of the British fleet. The mystery of the whole affair was the source of LaMotte's information, whose identity he refused to divulge, and throughout the trial this person was called the "friend in a certain office." The gossips of the day pointed their finger at Lord George Germain's protégé, Benjamin Thompson. No proof is available that the gossips were right, but it is interesting that Thompson suddenly turned over his post as Under Secretary of State for the Northern Department to a friend and left abruptly for America.

If Thompson was in fact spying on the British Navy for the French, Lord Sandwich, the First Lord of the Admiralty, would certainly have put pressure on Parliament to discover the "friend in a certain office," and it may well have been that the information which we know Thompson himself had gathered on the inefficiency and stupidity in Admiral Hardy's fleet was used by Germain to blackmail Sandwich into silence. Certainly, the "friend in a certain office" made out better than poor La-Motte, who was drawn and quartered at a ceremony of great pomp and popularity.

CHAPTER 5

Officer of the Dragoons

King George III was conspicuously unsuccessful in attracting and keeping competent ministers in his government. His reign was characterized by the maneuverings of a succession of high-ranking politicians bent on keeping their own jobs, often at the expense of their country's welfare. Anyone in Benjamin Thompson's position held his job only so long as his patron was in power, and every clever courtier tried to feather his nest by arranging some permanent position to fall back on when and if his patron dropped from favor. Thompson's scheme involved the formation of the King's American Dragoons.

The organization of military units under the sponsorship of aggressive politicians was an accepted, though highly speculative and expensive, procedure. It involved obtaining a Royal Charter for the regiment, raising the regimental strength at essentially no cost to the government, and finding a commanding general willing to use the military unit. The size of the unit determined the rank which the organizer might demand. Although the conditions to be fulfilled in such an arrangement were extremely difficult, the payoff tempted the gamblers, because when such a regiment was no longer useful to the military establishment, the of-

ficers were in line to keep their rank and go on
half pay for the rest of their lives.

The Economics of Raising a Regiment

It is rather difficult to unravel the real history of
the King's American Dragoons, not for lack of
documentary evidence, but from the fact that much
of the evidence comes from Benjamin Thompson
himself. We know that Thompson loved to exag-
gerate his own accomplishments, which makes it
difficult to sort out the truth from Thompson's self-
serving claims. One of the affairs that Major
Thompson had busied himself with when he fled
from Woburn to Boston was the recruiting of Loyalist sympathizers in Boston for a company in the
King's service. Thompson asserted, at least when
he got to London, that he had been promised the
rank of lieutenant colonel in this Loyalist brigade
if his recruiting should be successful. As he became wealthier under Germain's patronage, his
plans for the King's American Dragoons crystallized into a real operation, and he persuaded a
Major David Murray to sail for New York and
actively recruit this cavalry regiment into existence.
If all had gone well, Thompson could have stayed
in London as Under Secretary for the Northern
Department, had his regiment in action in America, and at the end of the war have reaped the
rewards of his military rank. If anything went
wrong with his plans, however, he had a ready
escape from whatever situation should arise, and
arise it seems to have done. In the summer of 1781,
as we have seen, Thompson suddenly found it
necessary to leave his comfortable situation in
London and apply himself to fulfilling the hard

conditions set down by the Crown for raising the King's American Dragoons to battle strength.

To indicate the magnitude of the job he had before him, let us look briefly at the conditions which he had to fulfill. He was to raise a regiment of three hundred and sixty-six enlisted men who were not otherwise occupied in any service for the King. The only expense of this to the government was the usual three-guinea bounty, roughly $10 in today's money, for enlisting. (Thompson more than doubled this out of his own pocket.) The officers were not to be other than "gentlemen of education and influence in America and have suffered in their property on account of their loyalty." By joining the regiment, commissioned officers gave up any right to claim pensions and allowances as "American sufferers." And lastly, no officer was to receive any pay until the regiment was half recruited; afterward officers were to receive half pay until the regiment was complete, when full pay would commence.

Two Skirmishes

Lieutenant Colonel Benjamin Thompson's military service in America was neither an episode of high adventure nor a demonstration of great military prowess. It was a stopgap affair aimed at building up the King's American Dragoons to fulfill his bargain so that he could claim his rewards. Although the ship that carried him to America was supposed to land in New York, contrary winds blew him south, and his actual port of debarkation was Charleston, South Carolina. During the months it took him to get to New York, he made himself useful to General Leslie, the British commander at Charleston, by leading a number of foraging raids out of the city. The only skirmish in which Thompson was engaged—that is, the only one important enough to be recorded—was against General Marion (commonly known as the Swamp Fox) in the marshes of South Carolina. In this encounter Thompson achieved his objective of gathering food and supplies for the British Army. When he finally found a place for himself and his horses on a transport to New York, he settled down with great vigor to the problem at hand, and not only succeeded in raising the full strength of his regiment of Dragoons but was able to arrange such a gala ceremony to celebrate its completion that the Prince of Wales himself presented the regimental colors.

The plight of an occupied town during the rigors of war is never an enviable one, but Benjamin Thompson left behind him in Huntington, Long Island, stories that equated the name of Colonel Thompson with the devil incarnate. He razed the village church and used its timbers for constructing fortifications, cut down all the apple trees for firewood although plenty of other wood was available. Adding insult to injury, he took up the gravestones and built baking ovens with them, and sent his soldiers around the town to force the natives to buy loaves of bread with the reversed epitaphs of their loved ones baked into the lower crusts. His only notable engagement while he held Huntington was to repel an attack by Benjamin Talmadge from the Connecticut shore, the details of which are minutely chronicled by General George Washington's informers, as well as by Thompson in his letter back to Lord George Germain in London.

CHAPTER 6

A Soldier of Fortune in Bavaria

The British made peace with the Americans in September 1783, and for months thereafter the port of London was choked with sailing vessels bringing back shiploads of refugees, each of whom felt that his particular claim of loyalty to the King should be rewarded. Joining the parade of favor seekers was Lieutenant Colonel Benjamin Thompson. The first hurdle he cleared was to get the King's American Dragoons transferred from an American regiment to a regular British regiment. He accomplished the transfer in a few months, and left for the records many pounds of paper explaining his rights and achievements. No sooner had he manipulated this transfer than he wrote to King George III, asking to be made a full colonel before retiring on half pay. The King's answer was, "I can see no real right to Mr. Thompson to obtaining the rank of Colonel which ought to be granted with a most sparing hand. Considering the few years he has served, that of Lieutenant Colonel seems very sufficient." Obviously, Thompson still had very powerful friends at Court; not more than three weeks after the King had written his demur, he promoted Thompson from lieutenant colonel to a full colonel. And with this rank in hand, finding

London still inhospitable to his aims and aspirations, Colonel Thompson left for the Continent.

Two Influential Contacts

A soldier of fortune seeking a position in the courts of Europe had to obtain preferment with a combination of luck, bluff, and the showmanship to make himself seem potentially useful. This was the sort of campaigning Benjamin Thompson was good at, and one has a feeling that he looked forward happily to spending a leisurely few months wandering around the courts of Europe seeking the best possible position. He made two contacts that had a considerable effect on his future. At Strasbourg, he spent time with the Duc de Deux-Ponts, whose regiment had fought for the Americans in the Revolution. Thompson's interesting tales of battles in the Revolution and his obvious acquaintance with its military commanders impressed the Duke's officers, who had been on the other side of some of the engagements which Thompson knew so much about. By the time Thompson left the Duke's camp, he had in his pocket the warmest possible letters of recommendation from the Duke to his uncle, Elector Karl Theodor, reigning monarch of Bavaria.

The second contact was with Sir Robert Keith, the British Ambassador in Vienna. The job of a diplomat in Central Europe, particularly in the seventeen-eighties, consisted mainly of trying to keep informed on the chaotic political status. One of the most useful functions a wandering soldier of fortune could perform was that of a political informer. Keith may have known that Thompson had already served several masters in this profession.

We do know that while Thompson was spending the winter of 1784 in Vienna, arrangements were made for him to pass along to Sir Robert all the political gossip he could pick up.

Sir Benjamin

Colonel Thompson's reception at the Court in Munich was beyond even his own optimistic expectations. The Elector of Bavaria treated him with great respect, and when Thompson offered his services as a military aide, the offer was accepted in most flattering terms. However, there were other officers in the Bavarian Court who would also have been highly complimented by the position which the ruler was offering to this foreigner. Some special qualification was obviously required, and Thompson, with his usual flourish, returned to London from Bavaria for the express purpose of persuading King George III that his position in English society must be at least equivalent to his promised social status at the Bavarian Court. It is a truly remarkable comment on Benjamin Thompson's hold over men to realize that he was able to persuade a king, who six months before was unhappy about raising him from the rank of lieutenant colonel to full colonel, to knight him as Sir Benjamin.

Bavarian Colonel

We can only guess why he succeeded. We do know that Thompson greatly exaggerated his family's status in society, for on his patent of arms he wrote, "Son of Benjamin Thompson, late of the province of Massachusetts Bay in New England, gentleman deceased, is a member of one of the most ancient families in North America, that an island which belonged to his ancestors at the entrance of Boston harbor near where the first New England settlement was made still bears his name, that his ancestors have ever lived in reputable situations in that country where he was born, and have hitherto used the arms of the ancient and respectable family of Thompson of the County of York, from a constant tradition that they derived their descent from that source." His emigrant ancestor may have come from York in England though the fact is not on record. We are sure, however, that his family never owned an island in Boston harbor. There does exist a Thompson's Island in Boston harbor, which showed on the maps of the day, but it was named after a David Thompson, who took over the island about 1626, whereas Benjamin's emigrant ancestor, James Thompson, did not come to the Americas until 1630.

There is a strong suspicion that part of the argument which persuaded the King to knight Sir Benjamin was for services promised as a British spy in Bavaria. Although we may never know how this stroke of genius was performed, almost for the asking Thompson received from the King of England what he wanted and returned to Bavaria to become aide-de-camp and confidential adviser to Karl Theodor, the ruler of Bavaria.

It is interesting to watch Sir Benjamin Thompson, now Colonel in the Bavarian Army, settle into his new surroundings in Munich. He had no particular command and no specific job except to do the bidding of the Elector, but he kept himself very busy. The records show that in the beginning he was as busy in spying for the British Foreign

Office as he was in his new duties. He made detailed plans with Sir Robert Keith in Vienna. "As we are acquainted with each other's handwriting, any signature in the future will be unnecessary, and though I should date my letters from Strasbourg or from Frankfurt, Your Excellency will not be at a loss to know from whom and from whence they come."

As time went on, however, his position in the Bavarian court became more secure and his urge to get ahead in his new surroundings became more important than his commitment to the British government. Keith, obviously eager to rely on such a strategically placed informer, became more and more annoyed when Sir Benjamin said that he could find out nothing, and Keith set other spies to watch Thompson. Their coded reports still exist in the British Foreign Office. If you like to match your wits against code, try deciphering the report on Thompson's activities shown in Fig. 4. (The decoded part of the letter is reprinted in the appendix at the end of this book.)

There is ample evidence to show that the Foreign Office was convinced that Thompson was holding out on them, which may explain an incident that occurred in 1795, when Thompson made his first visit to London in the eleven years since he entered the service of Karl Theodor. He was set upon by "highwaymen" in broad daylight in the middle of St. Paul's churchyard, and a trunk containing all his personal papers and documents was taken from him. Thompson himself believed that this incident was engineered by his political enemies, and it may well have been that the Foreign Office was so convinced that information he had gained would be of vital use to them that they went

No 20.   Munich 17th April 1788

My Lord

                    Since I had last
the honor of writing to your Lordship
The Election has dissolved the Commission
for examining General Sir Benjamin
Thompson's plan & they have been paid
according to their several ranks.
It is said they are exceedingly surprised
& disapointed as they were in hopes of
having the whole execution of the project
intrusted to them —— General Pappenheim
is returned here with his family under
the same expectations or with the
hopes of being appointed Minister de la
Guerre, but I have no reason to think.
The Marquis of Carmarthen ——
        &c. &c. &c.

course of the current year. ——

The new Prussian Envoy General Comte de Brühl arrived here the night before last & will probably have his publick reception & audience in a few days. as the Baron de Gemmingen had an audience to day to present his letters of recall. —

The Comte de Pritzenheim the Electors natural Son is going to be married to the youngest daughter of the Prince of Öttingen Spielberg.

1453. 2271. 1904. 174. 393. 122. 3061.

3736. 1123. 334. 3884. 3202. 3364: 1998.

74. 77. 1334 535. 2843. 2439. 2983.

1281. 406. 647. 2763. 576. 1510. 456.

1795. 787. . 685. 1264. 576. 909.8

2738. 9. 1396. 861. 678. 685. 2442.

2558. 1683. 2472. 566. 1330. 921.

809. 2954. 678. 646. 566. 3395

468. 1013. 2659. 3388. 1618. 2594.

3148. 1554. 4. 5887. 2487. 647. 599.

456. 1549. 129. 1396. 2760. 324. 2209

1798. 463. 53. 576. 1504. 1008. 693

3129. 1928. 253. 1584. 2760. 779. 288.

227. 1537. 367. 1618. 2457. 599. 678

458. 2993. 1618. 1793. 2193. 3364.

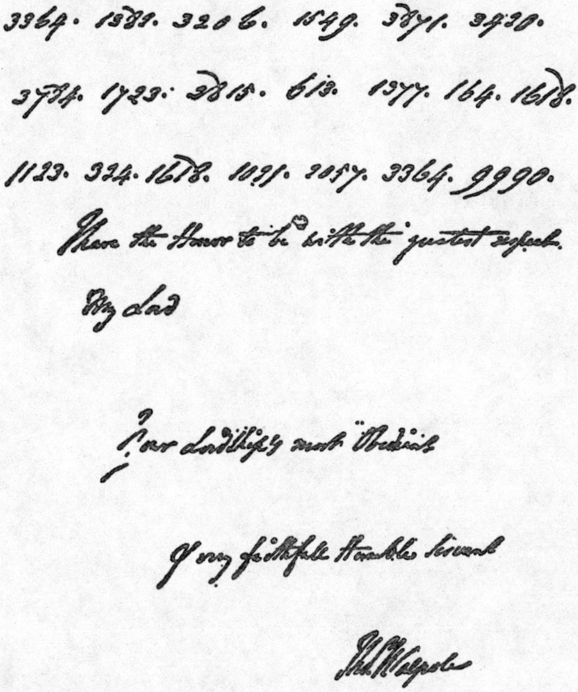

3364. 1581. 3206. 1549. 3871. 3420.

3784. 1723. 3815. 613. 1377. 164. 1618.

1123. 324. 1618. 1091. 3057. 3364. 9990.

Have the Honor to be with the greatest respect.

My dead

Your Lordships most Obedient

& very faithfull Humble Servant

Thos Walpole

Fig. 4. British secret code report on Benjamin Thompson's activity in Munich.

to these lengths to look at his possessions. It is fascinating to think that these papers may still be in existence in the original trunk taken from his carriage, still lying hidden away in some castle storeroom.

CHAPTER 7

Court Life and Research

Up to the time that Benjamin Thompson became the aide-de-camp to the Elector of Bavaria, his military and political fortunes had been his main interest, and everything he did was directed toward acquiring fame and fortune in these fields. As he settled into the court routine in Munich, his characteristic restlessness began to leave him, and more and more he turned his attention to scientific and technological questions which were to bring him in the field of applied science a lasting fame far beyond either his military accomplishments or his political stature.

The Bavarian Army was numerically large but almost useless as a fighting force because its organization was so poor, its morale so low, and its soldiers so ill-equipped. The Bavarian Court stood in constant fear of aggression from without and disintegration of the Army from within. On top of this, it cost the Elector of Bavaria a large fraction of his wealth to keep his Army from falling apart altogether. Colonel Thompson's real job seems to have been that of confidential adviser to the Elector of Bavaria, with the idea of recommending and carrying through reorganization of the Army by whatever means he found possible to use, with the stipulation that it was to cost the Bavarian government no more money than was customarily raised for the military war chest. If improvements were made in such a fashion that the Army became better and more effective, and this could be done at less expense than before, Sir Benjamin could have for his own use the money thus saved.

For several years nothing startling appeared to be happening in Munich, and most people forgot the dashing young colonel from Massachusetts who seemed to have been swallowed up by the courtier's life in Munich and Mannheim. Thompson, however, was extremely busy. He studied the organization of the Army in its most intimate details. He analyzed the problems of supply and accoutrement down to the last shoe. And he drew up a plan of reorganization so comprehensive that his detractors and ill-wishers were to be overwhelmed by the expanse and completeness of the scheme. Although many of the details were so specific to the Bavarian Army that we need not dwell on them, his mode of operation was so modern in its concept that only very recently have government-sponsored research and development caught up with the pattern which Benjamin Thompson set in the late seventeen-eighties as a blueprint for technological innovation. Thompson's startling new concept was this: For maximum result in minimum time, scientific insight must precede technological development. We shall see illustrations of Thompson's method of operation throughout this book.

When he analyzed the military budget, it became obvious that the two largest items of expenditures were the soldiers' food and clothing. Thompson posed himself two questions. First, were the soldiers wearing the best possible kind of clothing? Second, could anything be done to reduce the ex-

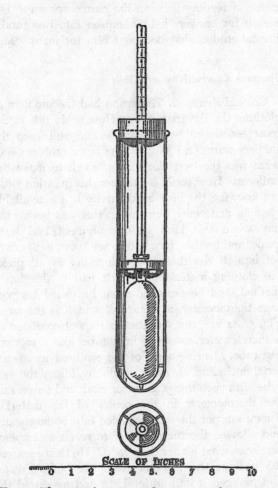

FIG. 5. Thompson's passage thermometer for measuring thermal conductivity of cloth and other insulating materials.

pense of feeding them in the customary way? The search for answers led Thompson into two fundamental studies that occupied him for many years.

Thermal Conductivity of Cloth

Colonel Benjamin Thompson had the problem of clothing the Bavarian Army. How to do this in the most economical way possible and still keep the soldiers warm and happy? The basic problem was, what was the best cloth from which to make the uniforms? How could he answer this question without knowing the heat conductivity of the available clothing materials? Remember, this was before the day when this kind of measurement had been made, and he therefore had to set about to discover for himself the thermal conductivity of all possible clothing materials. He first had to develop a method, and he designed what he called his passage thermometer, a picture of which is shown in Fig. 5. As you can see, the instrument consisted of a thermometer mounted in a tube like a modern test tube. Measurements of the conductivity of material including air were made by filling the test tube with such things as fur or cloth and immersing the thermometer in the center of the material. Thompson put the whole device into boiling water and allowed the thermometer to reach a temperature somewhat higher than 70° C. He then removed the passage thermometer from the boiling water and plunged it into an ice bath and measured the length of time it took the thermometer to fall from 70° C to 10° C. This length of time, therefore, gave him a measure of the rapidity with which heat passed through his test material.

First, he went through a study of all the common

substances used for warm clothing and carefully tabulated these in terms of their thermal conductivity. He tried to develop a theory which would explain the results and, hopefully, would give him a guide for choosing proper materials for the soldiers' uniforms. Thompson was first impressed by the fact that fur and feathers had better insulating properties than plain air. He wound his thermometer tightly with silk thread and found that the insulation of the silk thread was not as good as raw silk merely stuffed into his passage thermometer apparatus. Reasoning from both kinds of results, he suggested the hypothesis that the layer of air adhering to the surface of the insulating fibers was responsible for their thermal insulation. While Thompson was in England in 1779, he had carried on a fairly extensive series of experiments on air adhering to vegetable and animal fibers; he had found at that time that air apparently adheres much more strongly to fur than to linen. It was this lead that gave him the idea that the adhering air might account for the phenomenon of thermal insulation.

As the number of his experiments increased, however, Thompson found no direct correlation between the thermal conductivity and the apparent amount of air adhering to the surface of a fiber, and he looked around for another explanation. Still puzzled by the insulating qualities of cloth, Thompson next wondered whether insulation was somehow connected with the absorption of moisture from the air by the fibers of the cloth. He found that dry air was a better insulator than moist air, and, reasoning that flannel worn next to the skin might derive its insulation properties from the drying effect of the flannel in absorbing body perspiration, he carried out a series of investigations to correlate the absorptivity of fibers for water vapor with their insulating properties. He published a paper on this subject, "An Account of Some Experiments Made to Determine the Quantities of Moisture Absorbed from the Atmosphere by Various Substances," beginning, "Being engaged in a course of experiments upon the conducting powers of various bodies with respect to heat and particularly of such substances as are commonly made use of for cloathing in order to see if I could discover any relation between the conducting powers of those substances and their power of absorbing moisture from the atmosphere, I made the following experiments."

In these experiments, using his passage thermometer, he measured the increase in weight of various substances after being exposed for seventy-two hours in a room where he managed to keep the relative humidity close to one hundred per cent. He measured the moisture absorbed in sheep's wool, beaver fur, the fur of a Russian hare, eider down, raw silk and silk ravelings of white taffeta, fine lint of linen and ravelings of fine linen, cotton wool, and even silver wire from the ravelings of gold lace. These experiments led him to the conclusion that there was no correlation between the moisture absorbed by a fiber and the thermal conductivity of cloth made of the fibers and that, therefore, he must search further for an explanation of the thermal insulation properties of cloth.

Thompson's Discovery of Convection Currents

None of Sir Benjamin's theories seemed to be valid, and, at the moment, he was stuck. But he pursued his experiments and shortly thereafter had his reward, a really first-class discovery. Quite accidentally he observed and properly analyzed what we now call convection currents, and he vividly described his discovery in the following words: "In the course of a set of experiments on the communication of heat in which I had occasion to use thermometers of an uncommon size . . . filled with various kinds of liquids, having exposed one of them which was filled with spirits of wine in as great a heat as it was capable of supporting, I placed it in a window where the sun happened to be shining to cool. When, casting my eyes on its tube which was quite naked . . . I observed an appearance which surprised me and at the same time interested me very much indeed. I saw the whole mass of the liquid in the tube in a most rapid motion running swiftly in two opposite directions, up and down at the same time. The bulb of the thermometer, which is of copper, had been made two years before I found leisure to begin my experiments, and having been left unfilled without being closed with a stopple, some fine particles of dust had found their way into it, and these particles which were intimately mixed with the spirits of wine on their being illuminated by the sun's beams became perfectly visible . . . and by their motion discovered the violent motions by which the spirit of wine in the tube of the thermometer was agitated. . . . On examining the motions of the spirits of wine with a lens, I found that the ascending current occupied the axis of the tube and that it descended by the sides of the tube."

Capitalizing on this discovery, Thompson carried out many painstaking experiments in the propagation of heat through all kinds of substances, gases and liquids primarily, and soon could state as a general principle that any substance which tended to impede the motion of a fluid, be it a liquid or a gas, increased the insulation properties of the material. Applying this conclusion to his original experiments on clothing, he properly deduced that if cloth were so woven and of such a material that air was trapped in the interstices of the fibers and could not move around as a result of convection currents, it would be a poor conductor of heat and thus a good insulator. It should be pointed out that the Thompson discovery of convection currents was immediately hailed by the scientific world as a major advance in understanding the operation of the mysterious substance heat, although the name we now use, "convection currents," was not introduced until many years later—by William Prout in 1834.

As a result of his discoveries and measurements, Colonel Thompson felt satisfied that he understood the principles upon which the warmth of cloth depended, and turned his attention toward using this knowledge in a practical way.

CHAPTER 8

Thompson as a Social Reformer

It was all very well for Thompson to carry out a fundamental research project on the properties of cloth in order to determine the best possible material from which to make the warmest soldiers' uniforms, but it obviously could not be translated into practical clothing without persuading manufacturers to use the conclusions of his scientific endeavors. As one might well expect, the manufacturers from whom the Bavarian Army bought its cloth did not like the idea that the materials they had been furnishing were not the best and cheapest, nor did they even understand the basic utility of Thompson's scientific investigations. It soon became evident to Colonel Thompson that if he was really to use his basic studies, either he would have to find manufacturers whom he could persuade or he would have to go into the manufacture of the uniforms himself. Persuasion turned out to be of no avail; he made no progress whatever in persuading the manufacturers of the Elector's uniforms to translate his experiments on the conductivity of clothing material into modification of the soldiers' uniforms. He had to decide whether to abandon the project or have the uniforms made himself. Never one to quit, he set up what he called a "military workhouse," in Mannheim, for the manufacture of uniforms. This move, of course, threatened a real loss of business for those who had been supplying the soldiers' clothing, and the industrialists of Mannheim put every conceivable block in the way of successful operation of the military workhouse. Their principal success was to prevent Thompson from getting workers, particularly people who knew anything about the process of making cloth, and his Mannheim workhouse was a marginal operation at best.

A Scheme to Put Beggars to Work

This setback, however, far from discouraging Benjamin Thompson, put him vigorously to work analyzing economics and searching for a solution that would be both practical and spectacular. He began to think about Munich's swarm of beggars, who made up five per cent of the population. Not only was the percentage of beggars incredibly high, but they were organized to a degree scarcely exceeded by the civilian control of the city. They had their leaders, their gangs, their areas of operation, and such a high degree of organization that alliances were made even by marriage to gain control of particularly wealthy neighborhoods of the city. So organized were the beggars that the city police dared not disturb their functioning, and lay and clerical groups restricted their giving to particular gangs. As one would expect, the full viciousness of gang warfare and hoodlum mobs was rampant in the city, and the beggars themselves plied their trade with no interference from civil authority. So entrenched had the beggars become through the years that beggar parents, without fear of reprisal or prosecution, would mutilate and deform their children to make them pitiable and thus more appealing to almsgivers.

Many social reformers had attempted to rid the city of this plague, but all failed when they ran up against the malicious beggars' organization and the timidity of the civil authorities. Beggars, of course, did essentially nothing, and Thompson, looking around for a labor supply not attached to the industrial scene, saw here a tremendous potential labor force. He conceived a plan so daring that it verged on the fantastic. He would set all these beggars to work in his workshop making clothes and shoes for the Bavarian Army.

Herding all the city beggars into a prisonlike military workhouse was one thing, but keeping them constructively busy and reasonably happy was an entirely different matter. Thompson knew he would not be successful unless his plan had a real advantage for the beggars themselves. A plan for a Poor People's Institute in Munich had been well under way for a number of years, and Colonel Thompson saw the possibility of combining his workhouse and the Institute; he would feed and clothe the families of his factory workers in return for their labor for the benefit of the Army. He tried to persuade the organizers of the Institute to join his grand scheme for tapping the beggar labor force. Unfortunately for them, they resisted being absorbed into Colonel Thompson's scheme, but Thompson, through intrigue and political maneuvering, not only managed to have all the originators of the plan fired but sued the director for misappropriation of state funds, and this poor man, Piaggino by name, publicly accused Colonel Thompson of hiring thugs to beat him into submission when he resisted the Colonel's persuasion. In spite of the questionable methods, Thompson succeeded in taking over the Poor People's Institute. With everything in readiness he chose New Year's Day, 1790, to put his master plan into operation, picking the day specifically because it was the traditional beggars' holiday in Munich. He himself put out the first hand to arrest the first beggar, and with the Army in force throughout the city, by nightfall every beggar and mendicant peddler in the city had been processed through the city jails.

Life in the Workhouse

Written instructions issued to Thompson's subordinates and essays published to advertise his plans have given us a good picture of the Colonel's strategy. To catch a little of the flavor of his writing and to show the depth of his planning as well as his understanding, we might read some of his thoughts as he himself gave them in his memoirs:

> By far the greater number of the poor people to be taken care of were not only common beggars but had been bred up from their very infancy in that profession, and were so attached to their indolent and dissolute way of living as to prefer it to all other situations. They were not only unacquainted with all kinds of work but had the most insuperable aversion to honest labor, and had been so long familiarized with every crime that they had become perfectly calloused to all sense of shame and remorse. . . .
>
> We must follow the people who were arrested in the streets to the asylum which was prepared for them but which, no doubt, appeared to them at first a most odious prison.
>
> As by far the greater part of these poor creatures were totally unacquainted with every kind of use-

ful labor, it was necessary to give them such work at first as was very easy to perform and in which the raw materials were of little value, and then by degrees as they became more adroit to employ them in manufacturing more valuable articles . . .

As the clothing of the Army was the market upon which I principally depended in disposing of manufactures which should be made in the house, the woolen manufactory was an object most necessary to be attended to and from which I expected to derive most advantage to the establishment. But since it was necessary to begin with the manufacture of hemp and flax, not only because those articles are less valuable than wool and the loss arising from their being spoiled by the awkwardness of the beginners is of less consequence, but also for another reason, which appears to me to be of so much importance as to require a particular explanation. . . . My employing the poor people in question at first in the manufactures of hemp and flax, manufactures which were not intended to be carried on to any extent, it was easy afterwards when they had acquired a certain degree of address in their work to take them from these manufactures and put them to spinning the wool, worsted and cotton, care having been taken to fix the price of labor on these last mentioned manufactures at a reasonable rate. . . .

Those who understood any kind of work were placed in the apartments where the work they understood was carried on, and the others, being classed according to their sexes and as much as possible according to their ages, were placed under the immediate care of the different instructors. By much the larger number were put to spinning of hemp; others, and particularly the young children from four to seven years of age, were taught to knit and to sew, and the most awkward among the men, and particularly the old, the lame, and the infirm,

were put to carding of wool. Old women, whose
sight was too weak to spin or whose hands trem-
bled with palsy, were made to spool yarn for the
weavers. And young children, who were too weak
to labor, were placed upon the seat directed for that
purpose round the rooms where the other children
worked . . .

At the hour of dinner a large bell was rung in
the court, when those at work in the different parts
of the building repaired to the dining hall where
they found a wholesome and nourishing repast consisting of about a pound and a quarter, avoirdupois
weight, of a very rich soup of peas and barley
mixed with cuttings of fine white bread, and a piece
of excellent rye bread weighing seven ounces,
which last they commonly put in their pockets and
carried home for their supper. Children were allowed the same portion as grown persons, and a
mother who had one or more young children was
allowed a portion for each of them. Those who,
from sickness or other body infirmities, were not
able to come to the workhouse, as also those on account of young children they had to nurse or sick
persons to take care of, found it more convenient to
work at their own lodgings, and of these there were
many, were not on that account deprived of their
dinners. Upon representing their cases to the committee, tickets were granted them upon which they
were authorized to receive from the public kitchen
daily the number of portions specified in the ticket,
and these they might send for by a child or by any
other person they thought proper to employ. It was
necessary, however, that the ticket should always
be produced: otherwise the portions were not delivered. . . .

I have already mentioned that these children
who were too young to work were placed upon
seats built round the hall where other children
worked. This was done in order to inspire them

with the desire to do that which other children, apparently more favored, more caressed and more praised than themselves, were permitted to do, and of which they were obliged to be idle spectators and this had the desired effect. As nothing is so tedious to a child as being obliged to sit still in the same place for a considerable time, and as the work which the other more favored children were engaged in was light and easy and appeared rather amusing than otherwise, being the spinning of hemp and flax with small light wheels turned with the foot, these children who were obliged to be spectators of this busy and entertaining scene became so uneasy in their situation and so jealous of those who were permitted to be more active, that they frequently solicited with great importunity to be permitted to work, and often cried most heartily if this favor was not instantly granted them. . . .

As constant application to any occupation for too great a length of time is apt to produce disgust, and in children might even be detrimental to health, beside the hour of dinner an hour of relaxation from work from eight o'clock till nine in the forenoon and another hour from three o'clock till four in the afternoon were allowed them, and these two hours were spent in school which, for want of room elsewhere in the house, was kept in the dining hall where they were taught reading, writing and arithmetic by a schoolmaster engaged and paid for the purpose. In this school other persons who worked in the house of more advanced age were admitted if they requested it, but few grown persons seemed desirous of availing themselves of this permission. As to the children, they had no choice in the matter. Those who belonged to the establishment were obliged to attend the school regularly every day, morning and evening. The school books, paper, pens and ink were furnished at the expense of the establishment.

As a result of his experimentation with the Military Workhouse and the Poor People's Institute in Munich, Benjamin Thompson is often credited with having been the first to introduce a public school system.

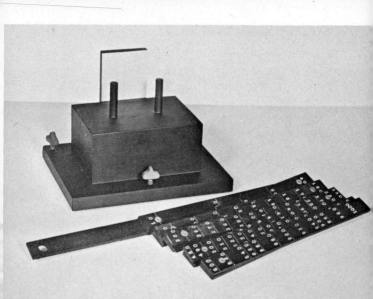

PLATE I (above). A Rumford photometer.
PLATE II (below). Experimental arrangement of the cannon boring study.

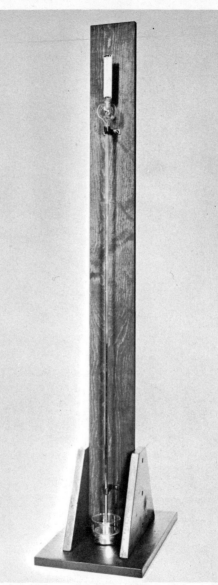

PLATE III. To measure the transmission of heat through a vacuum, Rumford mounted a thermometer in the top of a mercurial barometer.

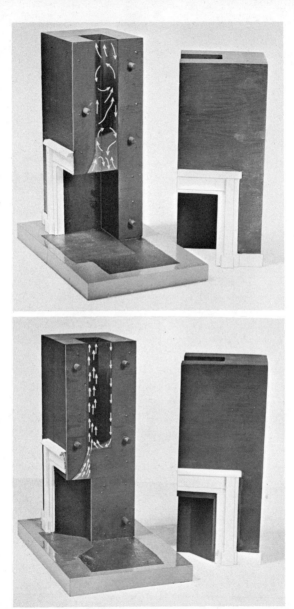

PLATE IV (Top). Model of a smoky fireplace. (Bottom) Model of a Rumford fireplace.

PLATE V (above). A model of a portable cooking stove.
PLATE VI (below). A model of Rumford's equipment for measuring the radiation properties of different kinds of surfaces.

CHAPTER 9

A Scientific Approach to Nutrition

The largest single continuing expense which Colonel Thompson had in reorganizing, equipping, and operating the Army was obviously the cost of food. Not only did he have the problem of feeding the soldiers, but in his enthusiasm to equip them from his own military workshops, he acquired the further responsibility of feeding the poor of Munich as well. Essentially no work had been done on the science of nutrition. In order to hold to his basic plan of first understanding the problem and then applying this knowledge to improvements, Colonel Thompson had to develop a standard menu that would be sufficiently wholesome to feed both his workers and his Army and that would cost the barest minimum.

One aspect of the scientific method of solving problems is to develop a hypothesis, test the hypothesis insofar as one is able, and then build a theory that will be accepted as correct until additional facts bring its validity into question. It is interesting to see in the development of science quite incorrect theories becoming the basis of scientific developments of great value. A case in point is Thompson's study of nutrition and his successful attempt to feed masses of soldiers and factory workers at an absolute minimum cost. There was at the time a fairly well-developed theory of plant nutrition which postulated that hydrogen and oxygen were the plant's basic needs and that fertilizers and manures did not feed plants directly but broke down the molecular structure of water, making available for the plant's nutrition the hydrogen and oxygen of the water. Thompson accepted this naïve theory and found many examples which demonstrated his contention that water, properly treated, was one of the most important ingredients of animal nutrition. In a long and careful study of animal feeding, he discovered that hogs and cattle put on more weight and were healthier if their feed was cooked into a gruel, so that the cereals and grains were boiled in large quantities of water.

Maximum Nutrition at Minimum Cost

Having persuaded himself that water was the fundamental ingredient of food, Thompson came to the obvious conclusion that soup would be the best possible form of food for the Army and the hundreds of people in his Military Workhouse and Poor People's Institute. For five years he experimented with various types of soups to find the particular recipe that would provide the maximum nutrition at the minimum cost. The basic ingredients of the soups which he finally developed were barley, peas, and potatoes. Although customarily the soups in Bavaria had some meat in them, his experiments demonstrated that the meat was not an impressively nourishing ingredient but only provided flavor. He demonstrated that a man doing hard physical labor could work happily and efficiently if fed not more than four and three quarters ounces of solid material in the form of a soup. His experiments also tended to corroborate his theory of nutrition; when he tried feeding his workers on five ounces of potatoes and a large amount of plain water, they all but starved, while the same weight of potatoes, peas, and barley cooked in water kept the workers completely happy. This furthered his (erroneous) belief in the concept that cooking the vegetables in the water broke down the components of water so that it could become nutritious of itself. Thompson also discovered that the rate at which the food was eaten was important. Food eaten very slowly was more satisfying than food eaten rapidly. Therefore, he introduced into his soups stale bread which had been fried crisp and had to be chewed a considerable length of time. This process of chewing slowed down the eating, and Thompson believed that it increased the nutritive value of the soups served in his mess halls. He found potatoes to be cheap and filling, but since they were not considered fit to eat in Bavaria, for a while he had to smuggle them into his kitchen. All the preparing of potatoes was done in a sealed room barred to all but some trusted cooks. It was not until after the potatoes had been used in the soups for some months that he confessed their use; thereafter, potatoes became a staple of the Bavarian diet, and in central Europe generally.

How to Make a "Rumford Soup"

Perhaps you would like to try making a Rumford* soup. Although his recipes were given in terms of bushels, since he was planning to cook for twelve hundred people at once, he did give the

---

* Benjamin Thompson was made a Count of the Holy Roman Empire in 1792, and he chose the name Count Rumford.

recipe for the acceptable amount for a working-man's dinner, a total of twenty ounces of ingredients. The quantities needed are: one ounce of pearl barley, one ounce of peas, three ounces of potatoes, one-quarter ounce of bread, one-quarter ounce of salt, one-half ounce of vinegar, and fourteen ounces of water. We quote from his own paper entitled "Of Food":

> The method of preparing this soup is as follows: The water and the pearl barley are first put together into the boiler and made to boil. The peas are then added and the boiling is continued over a gentle fire about two hours. The potatoes are then added (having been previously peeled with a knife or having been boiled in order to their being more easily deprived of their skins) and the boiling is continued for about one hour more, during which time the contents of the boiler are frequently stirred about with a large wooden spoon or ladle in order to destroy the texture of the potatoes and reduce the soup to one uniform mass. When this is done the vinegar and the salt are added, and last of all, at the moment it is being served up, the cuttings of bread. . . . It is of some importance that can well be imagined that this bread, which is mixed with the soup, should not be boiled. It is likewise of use that it should be cut as fine or thin as possible, and if it is dry and hard, it will be so much the better . . . for it renders mastication necessary and mastication seems very powerfully to assist in promoting digestion. It likewise *prolongs the duration of the enjoyment of eating,* a matter of very great importance indeed and which has not hitherto been sufficiently attended to.

Rumford soups became very famous throughout all of Europe, and one can still find them in continental cookbooks. His soups, however, were not the only things he recommended for his soldiers, and in his essay on food he produced quite a collection of nourishing diets, recommending such things as Indian pudding, apple pudding, a recipe for making a kind of macaroni called tagliati, various ways of cooking potatoes, such as boiling and baking, potato dumplings, potato salad, brown soup made of rye bread, and so on. In one of these essays he instructs his reader in the details of chewing to make sure that all the solid material of the food is carefully mixed with liquids before it is ingested into the body.

CHAPTER 10

The Versatile Inventor

The Bavarian Army, which was numerically large but poor in both money and equipment, had a serious morale problem—the soldiers had practically nothing to do. Almost universally illiterate, they could not even read to while away the time. Soldiers continually got themselves and their communities in trouble in rebellion against the sheer boredom of the soldier's life. One of the outstanding changes Thompson initiated in his reorganization of the Army was a concentrated attack on this problem of the soldiers' idleness. Since most of the soldiers had come from rural backgrounds and would return to their farms after they had served their term in the Army, to train them to be better farmers would have the twofold advantage of keeping them occupied and improving the country's agriculture. For Colonel Thompson such a scheme would have an even greater advantage. If, under the guise of military and social reform, soldiers could be induced to grow their own food, the Army obviously would save a lot of money.

It did not take Thompson long to implement the plan. By order of the Elector, each garrison in the country acquired a garden, and the soldiers were set to work growing the food not only for their own garrisons but for the Military Workhouse and the

Poor People's Institute as well. The stimulus to agriculture became particularly useful after Thompson discovered that potatoes were the cheapest and most nourishing base for his soups. Since the potato was essentially unknown in Bavaria, the only way he could count on a supply of this important ingredient was to have it grown at his own command.

When working these military gardens became an established routine for the Army, Colonel Thompson was accused of ruining the military establishment, wrecking discipline, and degrading the soldiers by turning them into common farmers and laborers. Always sensitive to criticism, he introduced into his planning two schemes which successfully quieted his detractors. He ordered that walls be built around the military gardens and that these walls should be constantly built and rebuilt in the form of earthwork fortifications as a training exercise for his military engineers. His second project, the English Garden, (Englische Garten) was spectacular in the extreme, and the populace, changing their tune from complaining that he was ruining the Army, acclaimed him as a great innovator and philanthropist. This story is worth telling.

Munich's English Garden

The Elector of Bavaria was a man who hated cities, and his first few years in Munich had been unhappy ones because he was confined to the bustle of city life, bound by the cares of state, and denied the freedom of the countryside. What made life tolerable for him was a great tract of virgin land full of wild game and known as the Red Deer Grassy Meadows. The Royal Forest Ranger took over this paradise as a private game preserve and hunting ground for the Elector's exclusive use.

After having tried out his military gardens in various places throughout Bavaria, and having set up a model in Mannheim which could be copied throughout Europe, Benjamin Thompson turned his attention to creating a military garden in the capital city of Munich. Here, however, he wanted to modify the strictly military nature of the garden. He decided to create not only an area for growing food but also a park that would attract public attention. When he looked around for a place for such a public garden and park, he saw only one area large enough, and eventually the Bavarian monarch gave up his private deer park so that Thompson could have space for the ultimate in municipal gardens.

After years of planning and construction, the English Garden justly earned its fame. It not only produced food for public institutions, but contributed to the pleasure of Munich's rich and poor alike. It also provided a central focus for the social life of the city. The area was laid out partly in formal gardens, partly in lodges and recreation areas, and it included, besides the gardens, a school for veterinary medicine, farms for the breeding of better cattle, and semi-wild areas for hiking. The grand promenade, a road running around the periphery of the garden, was six miles long—an indication of the park's size. The park became world-famous, and part of it exists in Munich today, a beautiful informal tract of hundreds of acres in the middle of a busy modern city. From every point of view, this achievement was a tremendous success and a real legacy to the future.

The Economics of the Kitchen

Closely associated with Colonel Thompson's attempt to find the most economical food for the soldiers and workers in his workhouses was his study of the economics of cooking the food. He quite correctly divided the problem into two parts, the type of fuel and the type of stove to burn the fuel in.

To study the type of fuel, Thompson invented a device for measuring the amount of heat given off when wood, charcoal, or coal was burned. At the time, the standard experimental method of determining the heat produced by a burning fuel was to determine what weight of raw material it took to boil a given quantity of water. Although the relative amounts needed of different types of wood to boil a given quantity of water seemed fairly well established, nobody could agree on the absolute amounts. Each experimenter obtained a different result because the loss of heat through such a large temperature change—from room temperature to that of boiling—was really the controlling factor. Thompson recognized this difficulty and for many years tried to devise some kind of combustion calorimeter that would measure actual heats of combustion.

In 1797 he had his instrument makers in Munich build a very large apparatus, made of copper and more than twelve feet long, which was a very expensive affair indeed. However, experiments with the apparatus did not yield good enough results to warrant publication of his measurements. Working on these ideas, however, Thompson later perfected a small combustion calorimeter, which is illustrated in Fig. 6, which is drawn from Thompson's own

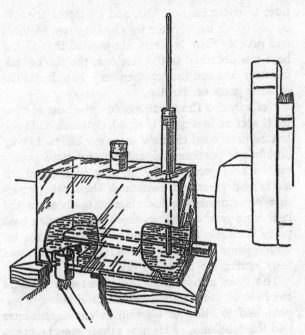

Fig. 6. Combustion calorimeter described to the French Institute by Count Rumford, February 24, 1812.

detailed description of this apparatus. The substance to be burned was held at the entrance of a flat copper worm mounted in a box full of water. The product of combustion passed through the worm and out the open end. The quantity of heat given off by the burning fuel was measured in terms of the temperature rise of the calorimeter. A special thermometer was employed whose bulb was as high as the water bath, to guarantee a good averaging of the water temperature. Thompson used his device over a ten-degree temperature rise, from five degrees below to five degrees above room temperature, to minimize heat loss, and he tested the efficiency of his calorimeter by building two of them and running them in series. He showed that all the heat was absorbed in the first one; the second calorimeter showed no temperature rise from the exhaust gases of the first.

Not only did Thompson measure the heat of combustion of various types of wood, charcoal, and coal, but he proceeded to study in a very elaborate way all kinds of possible fuel, and wrote various papers on the heat produced by burning fuel in various states of dryness and dampness. The most spectacular experiment was his attempt to measure the heat from combustion of ether—"an explosion took place from the vapour of ether kindled in the air with a flame that rose to the ceiling. Indeed it was near setting the house on fire."

Thompson also used this calorimeter to measure the heat of condensation of a large number of vapors, and to attest to his skill as an experimenter and the excellence of his new calorimeter, he measured the heat of condensation of steam to be 1040 B.T.U.,* which is within seven per cent of the value to be found in our present-day textbooks.

In Thompson's day it was customary to cook in front of a blazing open fire, and as he himself pointed out, the custom tended to "cook the cook more than the food." The greatest single improvement he made in cooking equipment was to enclose the fire in an insulated box, thereby inventing the form of stove which we now call the kitchen range. He spent a great deal of time designing kitchens for his military workhouses and for many

* One British Thermal Unit (B.T.U.) is the quantity of heat which must be supplied to one pound of water to raise its temperature one Fahrenheit degree.

hospitals, orphanages, and other public institutions all over Europe. All his stoves, however, were characterized by the novelty of enclosed fireplaces and looked not unlike modern kitchen stoves. His design for the Military Workhouse in Munich is shown in Fig. 7, and you can readily appreciate the tre-

FIG. 7. The kitchen stove in the Military Workhouse in Munich.

mendous change from open fires to this more efficient unit. Thompson's work on kitchen equipment was prolific. He invented the double boiler, the kitchen range, the baking oven, the fireless cooker, and advocated and introduced the use of the pressure cooker, for example, and one could write a book on this particular facet of Thompson's interest. So far as our interest here is concerned, however, we note in passing that his attempt to be economical in his feeding of the soldiers and of the poor had a tremendous effect on the culinary habits of the civilized world, since his inventions were largely responsible for introducing our forefathers to present-day methods of cooking and baking.

Measuring the Intensity of Light: Rumford's Photometer

Before we leave the subject of Thompson's improvements for the benefit of his military workhouses, we should turn our attention briefly to his study of light.

It is almost impossible for those of us brought up in the modern world to imagine how incredibly bad the sources of artificial light were before the early nineteenth century. Both rich and poor used wax and tallow candles. Although whale and vegetable oil lamps were well known to give considerably more light than candles, they burned with an appalling odor and were often so poorly designed that they constituted a very real hazard. The need for improvement in lamps or candles came home to Thompson when he was establishing his houses of industry for the poor in Munich and Mannheim. In these great, old, prisonlike buildings, with their tiny windows and crowded rooms, men, women, and children labored twelve to fourteen hours a day, many of them at arts and crafts that required careful concentration on detail. The loss of productivity resulting from poor light was sharply contrary to Thompson's religion of order and efficiency, and, with his characteristic thoroughness, he set himself to improve the situation. First he had to invent a device to measure the intensity of a light source, and developed what is to this day called a Rumford photometer. A model of this instrument is shown in Plate I. Let us read Thompson's own description of this device, which he calls "a very simple Contrivance for measuring the Intensity of the Light emitted by Lamps and Candles and other luminous Bodies":

A few words will be sufficient to give such clear and distinct ideas of the nature of these experiments and of the manner of performing the various operations they require as would enable any intelligent person not only to construct the necessary apparatus, but also to use it with the greatest facility and success.

Three tables will be necessary in making these experiments: on one of them the photometer is to be placed, and on each of the others, one of the lights that are to be compared. The heights of these tables should be such that the two flames of the lamps or candles that are to be compared and the centre of the field of the photometer may be at the same horizontal level. . . .

Suppose now that it were required to determine the relative intensities of the light emitted by two candles, the one made of wax, the other of tallow. The three tables are first to be placed at the distance of about eight feet from each other in the middle of the room or as far as possible from its walls, the photometer, elevated to a proper height, being placed on one of these tables, and one of the candles on each of the two others. The observer is now to seat himself before the table on which the photometer is placed and with his back turned to the two other tables. He will find two shadows of the field of the photometer and . . . the shadows must be brought to be the same density. This may be done either by moving the stronger light farther off or by bringing that which is the most feeble nearer to the photometer.

As the two shadows are reciprocally illuminated by the two lights, it is perfectly evident that the shadow which is least illuminated or of the darkest

shade must belong to the feeblest light, provided
the light be at the same distance from the field of
the photometer. But, as the intensity of the light
emitted by luminous bodies decreases as the distance from the source of that light increases, on
removing the stronger light to a greater distance
the intensity of its illumination at the field of the
photometer will be diminished, and the two
shadows may be brought to be of the same density.

In that case it is quite certain that the intensity
of the light *at the field of the photometer* cannot
be greater on one side than on the other. And, in
order to ascertain the relative intensities of the light
emitted by the flames of these candles, we have
only to compare the distances of those flames from
the centre of that field, for those intensities must
necessarily be as the square of those distances,
which is a fact too well known to require any il-
lucidation.

Instead of the rods divided into inches and
tenths of inches which I formally used for measuring these distances, I now employ flat rulers divided in *degrees*, which indicate directly and without any computation the relative intensities of these
lights.

These two flat rods which serve as a graduated
scale to the photometer are about one inch in width
and near one-quarter of an inch in thickness. They
may be folded up by means of joints, like a joint
rule, and the length of each of them may be about
ten or twelve feet. Their first division is marked
10° and it is placed at the distance of ten inches
from the middle of the field of the photometer
when the apparatus is prepared for making an
experiment.

The other divisions of this *scale of light* are determined in such a manner that the numbers which
they bear, which I call *degrees*, are everywhere *as
the squares of their distances from the middle of*

the field of the photometer, where the two shadows are in contact whose densities are compared and equalized.

To fill the important office of a *standard light* with which all others are compared, I have chosen a wax candle of the first quality, just eight-tenths of an English inch in diameter and which when burning with a clear and steady flame has been found to consume very uniformly one hundred and eight grains Troy of wax per hour.

This standard candle, which Thompson described while trying to improve the light for his workers, became for over a century the international standard candle, described in precisely the way that he described it in 1790.

Improved Lamps

Having discovered a method of measuring the intensity of light given off by various substances, he indefatigably went through a tremendous range of light sources, using both candles and lamps, to describe the amounts of light which they produced in terms of the amounts of material each consumed, and, hence, the cost.

The greatest single invention in the history of oil lighting had been made, in 1782, by a Swiss distiller named Ami Argand. His original invention was a lamp in which the air was drawn to the flame by a hollow, cylindrical wick. The air stream rose on the axis of the wick. Argand found that if he put a transparent chimney of glass around the wick, he obtained the brightest lamp known up to that time. Although these lamps gave the most brilliant illumination of any then known, they were complicated to build and the oils were expensive compared with wax and tallow candles. Thompson, therefore, set about to determine whether lamps or candles would be the most satisfactory form of light in his great institutions. He first measured the loss of light in the glass chimney of an Argand lamp by measuring the absorption of similar sheets of glass, and found the loss of light twelve per cent when the glass was clean, but more than double when the glass was "a very little dirty." The Argand lamp consumed considerably more oil than those of more common construction, but when Thompson related the amount of oil used to the intensity of the illumination produced, he found that a saving of fifteen per cent was achieved by the use of this newer lamp. He carried on an investigation "of the relative quantities of beeswax, tallow, olive oil, rape oil [from an herb of the mustard family], linseed oil, consumed in the production of light," and comparing the costs of these with their luminous output, found that rape oil in an Argand lamp with a very clean chimney gave the greatest efficiency. Subsequently, Thompson turned his attention to designing better lamps himself, but this, as you will see in Chapter 17, was many years later.

He made one further scientific advance in this period worth mentioning here. The caloric theory of heat was generally accepted, and it was common to consider light as a substance and one of the chemical products of combustion. In a paper entitled "Of the Light Manifest in Combustion," Thompson refutes this part of the caloric theory and shows that the light from candles and lamps results from the incandescent solid particles. He arrived at the general conclusion that the higher the temperature of these particles, the greater the intensity of the light. His description of the light coming from a candle is still the accepted explanation of the yellow luminous part of a candle flame.

CHAPTER 11

Sir Benjamin Becomes Count Rumford

While Thompson was busily engaged in his great reorganization projects for the Army and for the poor people of Bavaria, his spectacular plans encountered remarkably little opposition. One has a feeling that many of the social and political leaders of the country felt that improvements were sorely wanted, but that if somebody had to risk his future in drastic reforms, it would better be an outsider, someone who could be blamed for failure and exiled from the country if a scapegoat should be necessary.

A Spectacular Rise to Power

In Thompson's first four years in Bavaria, very little was done; he had to study the problems and work out the details of his schemes. Then from around 1788 to 1791 he actually put his ideas into operation, and honors flowed to him from every side. From a colonel in the Bavarian Army and aide-de-camp to the Elector, Thompson very rapidly rose to Minister of War, Minister of Police, Major General, Chamberlain of the Court, and State Councillor, holding all these offices at once, so that he became the most powerful man in Bavaria, second only to the Elector. Even the King of Poland climbed on the bandwagon, decorating General Thompson with the Order of St. Stanislaus, with the rank of the White Eagle. This sudden fame and fortune, however, made the other Bavarian leaders restless and fearful that the concentration of so much power in Thompson's hands would lift his soaring ambitions beyond outside control. Since Thompson's personality was such that he never tried to disguise his dislike for anyone in a station inferior to his own, his enemies multiplied rapidly. The Bavarian Archives are full of documents chronicling General Thompson's battles with other members of the Bavarian Court.

One of the most amazing of these incidents was provoked by an expression of popular gratitude to Thompson for his already famous English Garden. A group of citizens composed an address of gratitude to the Elector for his encouragement of Benjamin Thompson's plan and for his gift of the private deer sanctuary. To make sure that none would miss Bavaria's appreciation of his efforts, Thompson had the address printed and circulated it about the streets of Munich for all the citizens to sign. The Town Council was much annoyed. They felt that this was a city affair and should have gone through their office, because the English Garden came under their jurisdiction. In fact, they were so angry that they threatened to take legal action against anyone who signed this document praising Thompson's great works.

In August 1790, General Thompson went to the Elector and protested that the Council was trying to suppress a statement that was written to the Elector praising him for his foresight. The Elector, very desirous of praise for himself and very much under the influence of his powerful friend Thomp-

son, took drastic action against the town fathers.
He demanded that every member of the Town
Council should immediately resign and, further,
should offer public apology by kneeling in front of
the Elector's portrait and begging forgiveness for
the offense. Think of the humiliation if in your town
or city some official like the Chief of Police should
force your Mayor and City Council or your Board
of Selectmen to kneel publicly before a picture of
the President of the United States and beg forgiveness for having insulted the Chief of Police!
You can readily imagine who the most hated man
in the city would be. The members of the Munich
City Council were forced to endure the humiliation
and not only were dismissed from their positions
but were deprived of their civil rights for life.
Thompson seemed quite satisfied with this disposi-
tion of the case, but the number of enemies produced by this affair multiplied as the story was told
in its intimate details throughout Bavaria.

Count of the Holy Roman Empire

Although popular resistance against Thompson's
innovations then began to mount, the Elector, Karl
Theodor, seemed not to hear the rumblings, and
heaped even more honors on Sir Benjamin's head.
In the complicated interplay of European royalty
there was a coalition among the royal houses of
Europe called the Holy Roman Empire, the vestig-
ial remnant of the once mighty empire founded by
Charlemagne. In the eighteenth century there were
still emperors of this empire, but their crowns were
no more than honorary, handed down through royal
lineages in a definite and prescribed way. In 1792,
the German emperor, Leopold, died, and before

the new emperor, Francis, was crowned, there was
an interim period in which the Bavarian Elector
acted as Vice-Regent of the Holy Roman Empire.
In this brief period he wielded the power of the
Holy Roman Empire, and was able to use his office
to bestow honors upon his friends. He seized the
opportunity to elevate Benjamin Thompson to the
rank of Count of the Holy Roman Empire. Thompson chose as his title the original name of Concord,
New Hampshire (Concord had first been called
Rumford), where he had first started his amazing
rise in society by marrying the wealthy widow of
Colonel Rolfe. Henceforth we never find him re-
ferred to as Benjamin Thompson but always as
Count Rumford.

About the time he accepted the rank of Imperial
Count, Rumford's health began to show the effect
of seven or eight years of intense labor. After Rumford had suffered a series of very serious illnesses,
the Elector suggested that he take an extended
vacation, and the Count went on a tour of northern
and southern Italy. He traveled for sixteen months,
and although recovering his health was his prime
concern, he spent much of his time advising leaders in Italy on reforms they could institute in their
public organization of hospitals and almshouses.
When he returned to Munich in 1793, his arrival
was a signal for the greatest celebration the city
had ever seen. Half the population of Munich gathered in the English Garden to pay honor to Rumford as their great benefactor, and he was hailed
by the almost two thousand inmates of the Military
Workhouse, who sang his praises for having lib-
erated them from the evils of beggary and set them
on the road to useful lives as workers in his factories.

Although Count Rumford's trip through Italy did

much to restore his state of health, he was never as vigorous thereafter, although he was not yet forty years old. Having set in operation his great plans, he turned his attention more and more to scientific research and to writing up his studies in both science and sociology. It was during this period that he carried out some of his most famous experiments in the theories of heat, and they became subjects of lively discussion in the scientific world of the day.

CHAPTER 12

Contributions to the Theory of Heat

Almost every physics book that mentions Count
Rumford credits him, as I said in the preface, with
having developed our modern theory of heat. This
interpretation is not completely accurate, and is a
somewhat sad commentary on the way textbook
writers copy, over and over again, from previous
writers without taking the trouble to examine the
facts themselves. Rumford did make major contributions to the understanding of the nature of heat,
but most of his experiments were directed toward
disproving the then current caloric theory. It was
only after our present ideas were fairly well understood that later physicists interpreted Rumford's
experiments as having proved that heat was a form
of energy.

The Caloric Theory

Count Rumford first turned his attention to the
theory of heat during the series of experiments he
carried out in England in 1778 on the force of gunpowder. The caloric theory of heat prevailing at
that time pictured it as a fluid free to flow into a
body when it was heated and out of a body when
the body became colder. The fluid had volume;
therefore, a hotter body expanded when the fluid

flowed in, and contracted when the fluid came out. The caloric theory of heat explained the known facts, and on its arguments scientists were able to predict many phenomena in advance of their experimental discovery. If you think of the terms associated with the physics of heat, you will discover that our terminology still reflects the hold this theory had on the thinking of physicists in the eighteenth and nineteenth centuries. We speak of heat's "flowing" from one body to another. We measure the amount of heat in "calories" and talk about the "quantity of heat" to be found in a body. We measure this "quantity of heat" with a "calorimeter." Until the advent of thermodynamics in the eighteen-sixties there was no tool in the hands of physicists with which they could decide between various conflicting theories concerning the nature of heat.

Since it was known that a great deal of heat was generated in the explosion of gunpowder, the actual propelling mechanism was considered to be the caloric fluid released as a result of the chemical reaction in the explosion. Thus, in his attempt to explain the force of gunpowder, Benjamin Thompson naturally turned to study in theory, as well as by experiment, the basic physics of the process. In the course of this work he was puzzled by the fact that when he fired his cannon without bullets the barrel always got hotter than when shot was actually fired from his guns. If the amount of heat in the explosion was always a result of the released caloric, then no matter what the circumstances of the explosion the amount of heat should always be the same. And this he found not to be true.

As a young man in Woburn, he had read Boerhaave's *Treatise on Fire* and knew that the theory of heat proposed by that author was that heat, like sound, was a product of the vibration of a body. Boerhaave's theory would explain Thompson's observations since the expanding gas of the explosions passed through the gun with a higher velocity when it was free than when it was impelling a ball. He concluded that the higher velocity explosions produced a higher frequency oscillation of the metal of the gun and, hence, a higher temperature. With this as a start, he went through life looking for experiments that would disprove the caloric theory and incidentally help to strengthen his belief in the vibratory theory of heat.

As we have seen, Count Rumford rose to the position of Inspector General of Artillery for the Bavarian Army. As such he was responsible for the production of the military guns and cannon. The engineering work at the arsenal in Munich provided him with a most fortunate opportunity for carrying out some remarkable experiments. In the most famous of his cannon-boring experiments he discusses the two rival theories: "If the existence of caloric were a fact, it must be absolutely impossible for a body . . . to communicate this substance continuously to various other bodies by which it is surrounded without this substance gradually being entirely exhausted. A sponge filled with water and hung by a thread in the middle of a room filled with dry air communicates its moisture to the air, it is true, but soon the water evaporates and the sponge can no longer give out moisture. On the contrary, a bell sounds without interruption when it is struck and gives out its sound as often as we please without the slightest perceptible loss. Moisture is a substance, sound is not. It is well known that two hard bodies rubbed together produce much heat. Can they continue to produce it without finally becoming exhausted? Let the results of experiment decide this question."

The Cannon-Boring Experiments

Rumford's experiment conducted for the purpose of disproving the materiality of heat was entitled "Sources of Heat Which is Excited by Friction." The paper begins with a bit of philosophy which is as true now as it was then. "It frequently happens that in the ordinary affairs and occupations of life, opportunities present themselves of contemplating some of the most curious operations of nature, and very interesting philosophical experiments might often be made almost without trouble or expense by means of machinery contrived for the mere mechanical purposes of the arts and manufactures. . . . Being engaged lately in superintending the boring of cannon in the workshops of the military arsenal at Munich, I was struck with the very considerable heat which a brass cannon acquires in a short time in being bored, and with the still more intense heat . . . of the metallic chips separated from it by the borer. The more I meditated on these phenomena, the more they appeared to me to be curious and interesting. A thorough investigation of them seemed even to bid fair to give a farther insight into the hidden nature of heat to enable us to form some reasonable conjectures respecting the existence or nonexistence of the igneous fluid [caloric], a subject on which the opinion of philosophers has in all ages been much divided."

According to the caloric theory, friction produced heat because the force between the bodies producing the friction squeezed caloric fluid out of the material. The common operation of making horseshoes was often pointed to as a proof of this possibility of squeezing out caloric. When a blacksmith started hammering the horseshoe, it became very hot, but after he had hammered it for a while, it became less and less able to give off heat, and when the blacksmith could no longer keep the shoe hot by hammering, he put it back into the forge and reheated it. Thereafter, he could again keep it hot by hammering. The caloricist maintained that when the shoe was put back into the fire, the caloric which had been squeezed out of the horseshoe was put in again by the fire, and, hence, the process could be repeated. It was, therefore, a definite prediction of the caloric theory that heat could not be produced in an isolated body continuously.

Thompson argued that if caloric could be squeezed out as heat, then it ought to be possible to demonstrate the squeezing during the process of boring a cannon. The metal turnings which came out of the center of the cannon during the boring process should show less heat capacity than the same original weight of the metal of the gun before it was drilled out. Thompson set to work to determine the heat capacity of the cannon before the boring began and also the heat capacity of the metal turnings which came out of the cannon in the drilling. His very careful measurements of these heat capacities showed that they were exactly the same and, hence, that no material heat was lost during the boring process.

The experimental arrangement which the Count devised for his final experiments on cannon boring is shown in Fig. 8 and Plate II. The first is a reproduction of the Count's own illustrations for his paper, and the second is a photograph of a model of this experiment. By boring the cannon under water

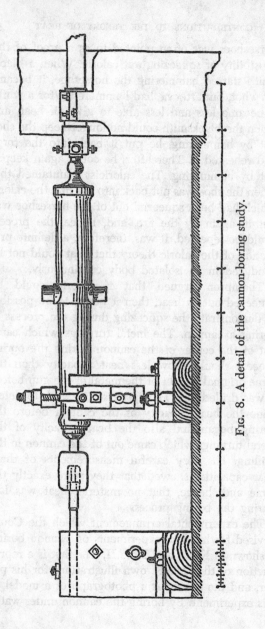

Fig. 8. A detail of the cannon-boring study.

and measuring the time it took the water to boil, he had a measure of the amount of heat produced. He found that no matter how long he kept the experiment going, the length of time it took the water to boil starting from room temperature was always the same, and hence he concluded that the quantity of heat produced did not seem to diminish no matter how long he kept the drill actually running. Apparently he did the experiment many, many times and loved to show it off to people. He wrote, "It would be difficult to describe the surprise and astonishment expressed on the countenances of the bystanders on seeing so large a quantity of cold water heated and actually made to boil without any fire. Though there was, in fact, nothing that could justly be considered as surprising in this event, yet I acknowledge fairly that it afforded me a degree of childish pleasure which, were I ambitious of the reputation of a grave philosopher, I ought most certainly rather to hide than to discover."

In his ever present desire to be considered a completely practical man, Rumford added two rather amusing notes to his discussion of these experiments. First, he pointed out very carefully that these experiments did not ruin the cannon, and that after the experiments were over the cannon could be bored in a normal way and still be used in the military arsenal. Second, he conceded that although a great deal of heat was produced by the borer, this was not an economical way of boiling water; if you should burn the fodder fed to the horses turning the drill, he pointed out, such a fire directly under the water would produce a great deal more heat and be much more efficient in the boiling process.

Beautiful as this experiment is, it by no means disproved the caloric theory of heat. The reason

why it is so often cited probably should be laid at
the doorstep of Professor John Tyndall. Professor
Tyndall was one of the most popular lecturers in
physics that ever lived. He was extremely influential in the teaching of physics in England, and he
made a triumphant tour of the United States in the
late eighteen-hundreds. He wrote papers on the
current problems of physics, and in one, entitled
Heat as a Mode of Motion, he reprinted Rumford's
paper on the cannon-boring experiment, comment-
ing, "Rumford in this memoir annihilates the material theory of heat. Nothing more powerful on the
subject has since been written." Obviously, however, this is a gross simplification. Rumford in his
paper asserted that his experiments had proved
that the heat produced by his boring was inexhaustible. This claim, as well it might, subjected him to
a good deal of contemporary criticism, since he was
extrapolating experiments lasting a few hours to in-
finity. And, in fact, one of his critics challenged him
to carry on his experiments until the cannon were
completely worn away before he could come to this
conclusion, a suggestion of which he took no notice.

There is no doubt that Rumford's carefully conducted cannon-boring experiment demonstrated a
real connection between heat and mechanical work.
However, he never gives us any indication that he
felt this connection was more than qualitative. The
quantitative connection embodied in measurements
of the mechanical equivalent of heat had to wait
for the brilliant theory of Sadi Carnot and for the
precise determinations of James Prescott Joule,
around 1850. That Rumford's measurements could
have been used to make this quantitative connection was pointed out by Joule many years after
Rumford's time. Joule used the Count's published

data to calculate the mechanical-equivalent heat from the cannon-boring experiment and came out with 1034 foot-pounds per B.T.U., a value within about twenty-five per cent of the presently accepted conversion.*

It was also Joule who pointed out that measuring the heat from mechanical work does not necessarily lead to an understanding of the nature of heat, any more than measuring the heat produced by an electrical current tells us of the fundamental nature of electricity.

Significance of Rumford's Contributions

These qualifications do not diminish the greatness of Rumford's contribution. His was a step in the right direction, but in the historical perspective one must be careful not to assume an insight into the nature of heat on Rumford's part which he himself gave no indication of having. He frankly did not understand the nature of heat, as he wrote of these experiments:

> By meditating on the results of all these experiments, we are naturally brought to that great question which has so often been the subject of speculation among philosophers; namely,—
> What is Heat? Is there any such thing as an igneous *fluid?* Is there anything that can with propriety be called *caloric?*
> We have seen that a very considerable quantity of Heat may be excited in the friction of two metallic surfaces and given off in a constant stream or

* The presently accepted value is 778 ft-lbs = 1 B.T.U.; that is, 778 ft-lbs of mechanical energy, when converted to heat, will raise the temperature of one pound of water one Fahrenheit degree.

flux in all *directions* without interruption or inter-
mission and without any signs of diminution or ex-
haustion.

From whence comes the Heat which was continually given off in this manner in the foregoing
experiment? Was it furnished by the small particles
of metal detached from the larger solid masses on
their being rubbed together? This, as we have already seen, could not possibly have been the case.

Was it furnished by the air? This could not
have been the case, for in three of the experiments
the machinery, being kept immersed in water, the
access of the air of the atmosphere was completely
prevented.

Was it furnished by the water which surrounded the machinery? That this could not have
been the case is evident: first because this water
was continually receiving *heat* from the machinery
and could not at the same time be giving *to* and
receiving heat *from* the same body, and secondly
because there was no chemical decomposition of
any part of this water. Had any such decomposition taken place (which, indeed, could not reasonably have been expected), one of its component
elastic fluids (most probably inflammable air)
must at the same time have been set at liberty, and
in making its escape into the atmosphere would
have been detected. But though I frequently ex-
amined the water to see if any air bubbles rose up
through it and had even made preparations for
catching them in order to examine them if any
should appear, I could perceive none, nor was there
any sign of decomposition of any kind whatever or
other chemical processes going on in the water.

Is it possible that the heat could have been supplied by means of the iron bar to the end of which
the blunt steel borer was fixed or by the small neck
of gun metal by which the hollow cylinder was
united to the cannon? These suppositions appear

more improbable even than either of those before mentioned, for Heat was continually going off or out of the *machinery* by both these passages during the whole time the experiment lasted.

And, in reasoning on this subject we must not forget to consider the most remarkable circumstance that the source of heat generated by friction in these experiments appeared evidently to be *inexhaustible*.

It is hardly necessary to add that anything which any *insulated* body or system of bodies can continually be furnished without *limitation* cannot possibly be a material *substance,* and it appears to me to be extremely difficult if not quite impossible to form any distinct ideas of anything capable of being excited and communicated in the manner the *Heat* was excited and communicated in these experiments except it be MOTION.

I am very far from pretending to know how or by what means or mechanical contrivance that particular kind of motion in bodies which has been supposed to constitute Heat is excited, continued and propagated, and I shall not presume to trouble the [reader] with mere conjectures particularly on a subject which, during so many thousand years, the most enlightened philosophers have endeavored, but in vain, to comprehend.

But, although the mechanism of heat should, in fact, be one of those mysteries of nature which are beyond the reach of human intelligence, this ought by no means to discourage us or even lessen our ardour in our attempts to investigate the laws of its operation. How far can we advance in any of the paths which science has opened to us before we find ourselves enveloped in those thick mists which on every side bound the horizon of the human intellect? But how ample and how interesting is the field that is given us to explore.

Further Experiments Designed to Disprove the Caloric Theory

One of Rumford's most ingenious experiments resulted from his unremitting search for disproof of the caloric theory; he tried to measure the weight of heat. According to the caloric theory, conduction of heat occurred because of a great attraction between matter and caloric. The less caloric a body had, the greater would be the attraction of its atoms for the caloric fluid. Thus, when heat was added to one end of a solid bar, the atoms at the heated end acquired more caloric than their neighbors, and having more, attracted the caloric less. The neighboring atoms would attract excess caloric away and would continue to do so until all the atoms in the substance had achieved the same caloric content. An attraction of any substance toward matter was considered to be a gravitational force. This theory predicted, for example, that denser bodies would have a higher conductivity than less dense substances. Benjamin Thompson himself carried out a long series of investigations under the title "Propagation of Heat in Various Substances," to show that the conducting power of substances of different forms and conditions had conductivities proportional to their densities, and that a single substance, when made denser, became a better conductor of heat. These experiments sound, at first glance, as if Rumford were busily carrying out experiments to prove the caloric theory of heat. Actually, however, this set of experiments was a preliminary one to convince himself of the facts, and having demonstrated that the greater the density the greater the conductivity, he drew a conclusion: If this theory were correct and if he should carry out his experiment in a vacuum, then in the absence of any material substance there should be no heat conductivity, because there would be no atoms to attract the caloric. Using the apparatus shown in Plate III, he demonstrated that if he evacuated the space around the thermometer, he could still transmit heat from outside of the vacuum to the thermometer suspended within, demonstrating to himself, at least, that heat apparently was transmitted without the aid of material substance, a fact which the caloricists could explain only with difficulty. Actually, to explain such experiments, the caloricists introduced the concept of radiant caloric, which was transmitted not by the attraction of material substances for the heat fluid but in the absence of material by a self-repulsive property of the caloric fluid. To which Rumford commented, "I must confess freely that however much I might desire it, I never could reconcile myself to [caloric] because I cannot by any means imagine how heat can be communicated in two ways entirely different from each other." We should point out, in passing, that this was very poor reasoning on Rumford's part, since there are *two* ways of communicating heat—radiation and conduction. Certainly his reasoning was not sufficient justification for rejecting a theory, however inadequate.

Since the explanation of many caloric phenomena was based on the alleged strong attraction between the caloric fluid and matter, many attempts had been made to measure the force between the caloric in a body and the earth—in other words, the weight of caloric. Count Rumford carried out a most clever experiment in an attempt to find the weight of caloric. He put water in one bottle, alcohol in another, mercury in the third, and hermetically sealed them. Each bottle weighed precisely the same. Rumford put the bottles in a room at 61° F and waited twenty-four hours for temperature equilibrium to be firmly established. He then checked the weight of his three bottles and found them still to be identical. Opening the windows of the room, he allowed the temperature to fall to 30° F, and then, by careful control, he kept it at this level for forty-eight hours. At the end of that time, his precise weighing of the bottles showed that they still were balanced when he measured them on his scale. He knew the specific heats of alcohol and mercury were very different and, therefore, the amounts of heat which the bodies gave up in cooling from 61° to 30° were different, being very much greater for mercury, with its large specific heat, than for alcohol. Despite these large differences in quantity of heat, no measurable difference in weight could be observed. The water, of course, had frozen and had given up a large quantity of heat in going from its liquid state to its solid state. This latent heat, though it was a very large value, did not change the weight of his bottle of water when compared with the weight of the bottle of alcohol, which did not freeze. Many of the physicists of the day felt that Benjamin Thompson went too far in his statement, "That all attempts to discover any effect of heat upon the apparent weight of bodies will be fruitless." However, no one was able to improve on his experiment and come to a different solution.

The expansion and contraction of bodies in heating and cooling were easily explained by the caloric theory if one assumed that the heat fluid had a volume. If a body were heated, the caloric took up

PLATE VII. An experimental lecture at the Royal Institution! Count Rumford is standing at the far right, and Humphry Davy is holding the bellows.

PLATE VIII. A Rumford student lamp with a tin shade in the Concord Antiquarian Society, Concord, Massachusetts.

PLATE IX. Photograph of a model of a Rumford steam heating system.

PLATE X (Top). Rumford's portable coffeemaker, ready for travel. (Bottom) Rumford's portable coffeemaker, ready for use.

space, and the body must necessarily increase in size. Similarly, when a body was cooled, the caloric was removed, and the body contracted. Searching for areas in which to attack the caloric theory, Rumford carried out a long series of experiments spread out over many years to demonstrate conclusively that water did not continually contract as it was cooled to its freezing point. He offered no theory which would explain the peculiar behavior of water, whose maximum density occurs at 41° F and which thus expands from 41° to 32° before it freezes. However, his object was to demonstrate without doubt a phenomenon that the caloricists could not explain.

Freezing and Contraction of Water

His experiment, which can be copied easily, was conducted with the apparatus shown in Fig. 9. The container, marked H, was filled with a water-and-ice mixture at 32° F. The tin ball, F, which had a conically pointed end, was cooled to slightly above 40° F. This ball was mounted as shown over the thermometer, placed in a cork cup, C. As the warmer water, about 40°, fell through the colder surrounding water, held at 32°, the cork cup filled up with this denser liquid and the thermometer rose from 32° F to 41° if the optimum conditions were established. It is obvious in this experiment, therefore, that the warmer water was falling through the colder and, hence, must have been denser than the colder. This apparatus became a fairly standard laboratory experiment for demonstrating the temperature for maximum density of water and was a real stumbling block to the caloric theory of heat. Rumford's conclusions were attacked

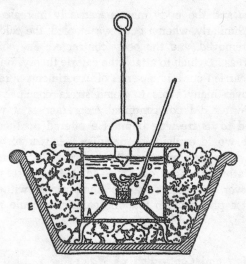

FIG. 9. Rumford's apparatus for measuring the temperature at which the density of water is a maximum.

vigorously by the natural philosophers of his day. The famous John Dalton, often called the father of the atomic theory, was one of his most severe critics, and wrote a long paper trying to prove that water did not become denser before it froze: "However keen and worthy of attention this experiment of Count R. may be, I do not regard it as conclusive as Count R. seems to do." In Dalton's long and fairly complicated explanation of Rumford's experiment, he tried to show that although the experimental observation was described correctly, the conclusion that warmer water was falling through colder was erroneous.

The natural philosophers who believed that the caloric theory of heat was a valid description of the facts felt that when a body was in temperature equilibrium with its surroundings, it was in a state of complete rest. That is, a liquid or a gas in an enclosed vessel at temperature equilibrium had all its atoms and molecules stationary in the caloric fluid. Those like Count Rumford who questioned this interpretation felt that there was a connection between heat and motion, and that somehow this motion was associated with the temperature of the body even in its equilibrium state. Rumford devised a very spectacular experiment to demonstrate this connection, one so simple and straightforward that anyone can try it for himself. What he did was to take two liquids, a salt solution and pure water, and put them in a glass container in such a way that the salt was on the bottom of the glass and the water on the top. He put the water in first and then introduced the salt solution below the water by pouring it through a funnel to the bottom of the glass. Then he dropped a single drop of oil of cloves into the glass. The drop sank in the water but floated on the salt solution, coming to rest halfway down the liquid column. The whole experiment was carried out in his cellar, where the temperature was constant, and he found that in the course of a few days the drop of oil of cloves rose slowly to the surface as their internal motions mixed the liquids completely. His experiment showed the internal motions of particles of the liquid continued even at temperature equilibrium, a phenomenon which should not occur under the caloric-theory explanation. Although he did not have a clearly developed picture of the modern kinetic theory of heat, his attempts to show that motion was an inherent property of a substance strengthened his belief that energy and heat were somehow connected. It is interesting to observe, by the way, that when the modern kinetic theory was worked out, it was Albert Einstein who pointed out that the spontaneous mixing of liquids of different densities affords one of the most direct experimental proofs of the predictions of this theory.

If you want to try this experiment yourself, you must prepare the salt solution of such a concentration that whatever you use for a marker, which Rumford called his "little signal," must not only float on the solution in its concentrated form but must also float on the solution at half that concentration; thus, when complete mixture results, your little sentinel will float on the top of the mixed liquids. Rumford used oil of cloves because it has about the right density; it is black and is very clearly seen, and does not mix with the water or the salt solution. Another way is to make these markers by blowing little hollow spheres of colored glass and choosing those which have the right density to work in this experiment.

CHAPTER 13

Success in England and Bavaria

Count Rumford's sixteen months in Italy gave him a chance to realize that a great many people wanted to hear about his scientific work and about application of his discoveries to improvements in living. On his return to Munich, he gave his attention increasingly to collecting data on the operation of his public institutions and to writing essays on all his physical and sociological experiments. It became important to him that he should publish his scientific work in English. Collecting his observations and ideas in pamphlet and book form would give them more of an impact than if he published them as individual papers in such learned journals as the *Proceedings of the Royal Society*. It was not easy to publish from Munich, and in the fall of 1795 he asked the Bavarian Elector to grant him another leave of absence. He returned to England to advertise the results of his eleven years' labors in the city of Munich. It was on his arrival in London that the already mentioned, most peculiar theft of his personal papers took place (see Chapter 6).

Rumford spent two years in the British Isles, and these were perhaps the happiest two years of his life. Wherever he went, people of consequence hailed him as a great philosopher and philanthropist. Everyone was eager to hear of his research and his improvements. He was invited far and wide to lecture, to advise, and to hobnob with the great. He was now a count in a land where the titles of nobility were important. Both society and science sought him out. People wrote poems and songs to his honor, and every journey became a triumphant progress. Amidst all the acclaim, Rumford remained a very hard-working man; he wrote and published industriously, and the public gobbled up everything he wrote. Any suggestion from his pen was taken as a great pronouncement, and his scientific theories were debated and defended even in the public press.

Rumford extended his thoughts on the inefficiencies of the Bavarian Army to the whole of society, and started to worry about inefficiencies and waste as a matter of principle, attempting to apply to society's ills the techniques he had used so successfully in Bavaria. Typical of his worries about waste was the attention he lavished on the problem of smoky chimney fireplaces.

Essay on the Improvement of Fireplaces

"The enormous waste of fuel in London may be estimated by the vast, dark cloud which continually hangs over this great metropolis and frequently overshadows the whole country, far and wide. For this dense cloud is certainly composed almost entirely of *unconsumed coal*, which, having stolen wings from the innumerable fires of this great city, has escaped by the chimneys and continues to sail about in the air 'till, having lost the heat which gave it volatility, it falls in a dry shower of extremely fine black dust to the ground, obscuring the atmosphere in its descent and frequently changing the brightest day into more than Egyptian darkness.

"I never view from a distance as I come into town this black cloud which hangs over London without wishing to be able to compute the enormous number of caldrons of coal of which it is composed. For, could this be ascertained, I am persuaded, so striking a fact would awaken the curiosity and excite the astonishment of all ranks of the inhabitants and *perhaps* turn their minds to an object of economy to which they have hitherto paid little attention."

It was thus that Count Rumford concluded his essay, "Chimney Fireplaces with Proposals for Improving Them to Save Fuel, to Render Dwelling Houses More Comfortable and Salubrious, and Effectually to Prevent Chimneys from Smoking." His essay on how to build fireplaces is one of the most remarkable of his writings because in it he outlined the principles of the efficient fireplace so completely that no essential improvement has been made in the design since his time. You will remember that, somewhat earlier, he had discovered convection currents and carried out the basic investigation leading to an understanding of the motion of currents of warm air. Using this knowledge, he introduced into the fireplace the narrow throat and smoke shelf which separated the hot air in the front of the fireplace from the cold air which must take its place in the back of the chimney. His improvements and the reason for them are well illustrated in Plate IV, which shows two models of fireplaces, one before Rumford improved them, and the other incorporating his improvements. Besides putting in the smoke shelf and throat, he also in-

troduced the damper for shutting off the outside
air when the fireplace was not in use. Furthermore,
he analyzed the flow of air, specifying the size of
the opening of the fireplace as it related to the
size of the throat and the drawing power of the
chimney.

Count Rumford also carried out a series of demonstration experiments to show that a fireplace
heated the room by radiation, and since very little
was known about the behavior of radiation, he went
back and did a series of fundamental experiments
to show that polished bodies did not radiate well,
but that rough, particularly sooty, bodies radiated
very well. The instrument he designed to demonstrate this effect is shown in Plate VI. His radiators
were copper boxes which could hold hot water,
and whose bottoms could take various surface cov-
erings, shiny metal or cloth or sooted surfaces. Between two such surfaces he put a differential thermometer, which he also had to invent and which is
well illustrated in the figure. The device is an air
thermometer, with a small column of colored liquid
for a marker. He rated the radiant power of his
surfaces, comparing the distance of the shiny box
when filled with hot water from one bulb of the
thermometer with the distance of an unknown
radiating surface from the other bulb of the thermometer. He adjusted the distances until the colored liquid indicator came to rest at the center of
the apparatus, equidistant between the two columns of air trapped on the two sides of the air
thermometer. He was able to show that good radiators were poor reflectors and vice versa, a fact
which was discovered almost simultaneously by a
British physicist named Leslie. The two men had a

spirited and at times vitriolic controversy as to who was the discoverer of this physical fact.

By various tests Rumford satisfied himself that he knew the way the heat of the fireplace was to be thrown into the room. He beveled the back and sides of the fireplace to maximize the radiation of heat into the room and recommended rough brick covered with soot as the proper material for the back and sides of the fireplace.

Rumford gave his best effort to his mission to reduce the smoke over London. He claimed the cure of at least five hundred smoky chimneys, two hundred and fifty of which he altered in a single two-month period in 1796. It became extremely fashionable among the social leaders of the city to brag that the famous Count had fixed their fireplaces. An amusing and popular caricature of Count Rumford warming himself in front of his fireplace came from the studio of the famous London caricaturist James Gillray. A reproduction of this print, which in its most expensive form was brightly colored, is shown in Fig. 10.

Fireplaces and chimneys, of course, were not the only things occupying Rumford's time between speaking engagements and triumphal appearances at social functions. He spent a busy two months in Ireland introducing his principles of economy and efficiency in hospitals and workhouses in that country; he worked to improve cooking stoves, both in public institutions and in many private homes throughout the London metropolitan area. A verse that appeared in the public press voiced the applause which the Rumford inventions enjoyed in London at the time.

Lo, every parlor drawing room, I see,
Boasts of thy stoves and talks of not but thee.

Yet, not alone my lady and young misses,
The cooks themselves could smother thee with kisses.
Yes, mistress cook would spoil a goose, a steak,
To twine her greasy arms around thy neck.

FIG. 10. A caricature of Count Rumford enjoying one
of his fireplaces.

The Rumford Prizes

In more serious vein, Rumford did another very
spectacular thing which benefits physicists today.
In 1796, he conceived the idea of setting up large

sums of money for encouraging research in the particular areas of physics which interested him the most, the fields of heat and light. He proposed to the Royal Society of London and the American Academy of Arts and Sciences, in Boston, that every two years each should award a medal for the outstanding work done in these two fields in the previous two-year period. To finance the awards, he gave each institution five thousand dollars. Although the stipulations which he laid upon the organizations were so difficult to administer that the American Academy of Arts and Sciences did not give a Rumford premium until forty years later, the value of the awards was never in question, and today these Rumford prizes are considered one of the highest scientific awards that a physicist can earn. The five thousand dollars given to each institution in 1796–97 has multiplied to such an extent that money is available from Rumford's original gift as grants-in-aid to research, as well as to cover the cost of the Rumford prizes themselves. Rumford medals were not given in America until long after the Count was dead, but the first Rumford prize from the Royal Society of London was presented to Count Rumford himself in 1802.

A Military "Battle" and Promotion to General

Count Rumford's pleasant and profitable stay in London was abruptly cut short in August 1796. An urgent request from the Elector of Bavaria summoned him back to his military post in Munich, and with the greatest possible haste. The French and the Austrians were at war. Europe was rapidly becoming a battlefield as the two opposing armies fought all along their borders and extended their

campaigns into neighboring territory. To get to
Munich, Rumford first had to sail for Hamburg,
then for three weeks make his way by carriage to
Bavaria with long detours to prevent his party from
becoming entangled in the opposing armies. When
Rumford finally got to Munich, he discovered that
Bavaria was very much in the path of the war, and
because the Bavarian Army had not fought any
battle for years, it appeared as if it could not protect its own neutrality. As we have seen, there was
no great love lost between the influential leaders in
Bavaria and the American Count, and by the time
Rumford appeared on the scene, the decision had
already been made that he was to take charge of
the Bavarian Army; the Elector and his entire
court would flee to Mannheim. Since no one had
faith in the Army's ability to take on either the
Austrians or the French, somebody whose political
and military future was expendable would have to
shoulder the responsibility for the predicted defeat.
Rumford's enemies had persuaded Elector Karl
Theodor to give this unenviable position to the
Count. Within a week of Rumford's appearance,
all the other responsible heads of state fled the
scene, and the situation seemed hopeless. As the
two best armies in Europe, the Austrian and the
French, converged on Munich, Rumford drew all
his men together and garrisoned them within the
city walls.

First the Austrians appeared, and Rumford persuaded them to camp outside the city. When the
French appeared on the other side of the city, Rumford hastened to General Moreau and persuaded
him that he had prevented the Austrians from en-
tering the city, and therefore there would be no
point in a French attack on it. For weeks the two

armies faced each other with General Thompson and his twelve thousand troops garrisoned in the city between them, and Rumford himself visiting first one army and then the other, negotiating day after day to prevent them from actually starting to fight, while he and his men were in the middle. Suddenly, one morning, the French packed up and left. Moreau had heard that another of the French divisions on the lower Rhine had been defeated, exposing his flank and so necessitating his withdrawal to shorten supply lines. With the withdrawal of the French, the Austrians retired to Vienna, and Rumford, who had been picked to take the rap as a defeated general, instead became the hero of Bavaria. This great victory, won without firing a single shot, was the only real military engagement Benjamin Thompson ever directed. He rose to be a general in charge of a country's army, having been in only two brief military skirmishes in his life before, one when he foraged for food in General Marion's territories in the swamps of South Carolina, and the other when he went ashore with a party from some longboats in Long Island Sound to skirmish with a Colonel Benjamin Talmadge under General Washington.

One of Rumford's plans to improve the city of Munich was to build a broad esplanade around the city, starting from the English Garden and encompassing the whole city back to the English Garden again. He discussed this plan with the City Councillors at some length, but their opposition prevented him from carrying the plan through before he left for England. You will remember that the City Councillors were vehemently opposed to anything that Rumford might suggest, and while he was in England, they constructed a number of public buildings directly in the path this esplanade would have taken. When Rumford returned from England, he found these spite buildings, which could have been built anywhere, already standing athwart his ideas for city planning. In preparing for the threatened battle between the Bavarians and either the French or the Austrians, Rumford used his authority to level all the land around the city, and took particular pleasure in blowing up the buildings which had been built to block his esplanade. Since, at the end of this incident, Rumford was the country's great hero, nobody dared to oppose his continuing plan to extend his park system, although his willful destruction of these buildings did not endear him to those who were already working to undermine his position.

Even when the fate of Munich rested upon his ability to protect the city from the French and Austrians, Rumford attacked the problem of feeding his entire Army and the citizens remaining in the city, and did it with typical attention to economy and efficiency. He ordered many experiments to be carried out to determine the best way to feed soldiers in the field, using the least amount of fuel and the most efficient type of portable stove. This started him on a long series of experiments on portable cooking utensils, a continuing interest through the rest of his life, but his major advances were made amid the harassments of a threatened population besieged by two opposing armies.

Invention of a Portable Field Stove

The standard equipment issued to the Bavarian soldiers for cooking meals in the field had been a three-legged iron trivet upon which an iron frying pan could be placed over an open fire. There was a fire for each soldier or for a small group of soldiers. While Munich was under siege, fuel became dangerously scarce, and any arrangement to conserve this essential commodity became not merely useful but almost vital. First, Rumford issued orders to throw away the open tripod; enclose a small fire on a U of three bricks. By this arrangement the cooking pot or pan was lowered to within a few inches of the ground, and a very small fire sufficed. This improvement, however, was only temporary. Following his previous principles, Rumford then set about to design enclosed fireplaces as tall as the old trivets the soldiers were accustomed to, but far more efficient in that the heat loss was cut way down by insulating the fire on all sides. A model of this type of portable fireplace is illustrated in Plate V.

In this hour of presumed peril, Count Rumford had somehow to feed not only the soldiers but the civilian population of Munich as well. Applying his principles of the mass feeding in his military workhouses, he designed and built field stoves according to his basic principles and set up soup kitchens for the whole city. These soup kitchens and the concept of feeding the soldiers en masse, instead of having each individual infantryman cook his own meals, became standard not only in the Bavarian Army but in military establishments all over Europe. Fig. 11 shows Rumford's own illustration of these portable kitchens, designed under the stress of war but based on a long series of experiments on the fundamental theory of heat insulation.

Count Rumford's spectacular ability to turn a hopeless military situation into another personal triumph dealt a staggering blow to the political

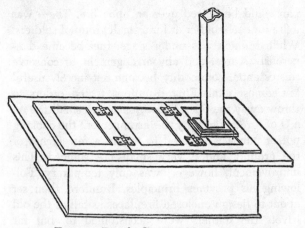

Fig. 11. Rumford's portable kitchen.

enemies who had hoped to use the city's plight as
a weapon to annihilate his stature. The success of
so remarkable a turn of events made them even
more vicious in their attempts to poison the Elector's faith in his American Count. It became obvious
even to Rumford himself that his usefulness to the
Elector was being badly damaged, and his future
on the Bavarian scene wilted as his political enemies hammered away at his position. Eventually,
Karl Theodor himself had to admit that the animos-
ity stirred up not only by Rumford's schemes but
by his annoying personality cut his value down to
a point where the Elector would have to dispense
with his services. He was loath to do this, however,
without arranging for a job which Rumford could
take with great honor, and, in 1798, he appointed
Rumford Minister Plenipotentiary to the Court of
St. James's, and sent him to London to replace the
Bavarian Minister. Contrary to the usual protocol,
the Bavarian government did not ask the British

government for its approval of the new Minister Plenipotentiary, and the consternation this appointment caused gave vent to an anguished howl from the circles around George III. The British King was furious that one of his own subjects, who already had been accused of spying against the British government, could be appointed Minister Plenipotentiary from a foreign country; he refused even to let Rumford try to present his credentials to any government official, and the letter he wrote to Karl Theodor about this affair so strained the relations between the two countries that they never again became cordial as long as Karl Theodor reigned.

CHAPTER 14

Rumford's Attempt to Return to America

Count Rumford, at the age of forty-five, found himself in London without a job. His plans for a brilliant
future as Minister Plenipotentiary from the Bavarian Court had collapsed, a very real disappoint-
ment to the Count. Apparently it had never entered
his mind that he might be unacceptable to the
British. So sure was he that this position of great
social prestige was his that he already had left Bavaria for a leisurely journey across Europe to England before George III had been notified of his
coming. His blithe anticipation of an enthusiastic
reception at the Court of St. James's made the open
hostility in official circles all the more bitter. But
his reputation among the public, and particularly
among the scientific and philanthropic people, was
still bright, and he set about to find, or create, a
position worthy of his talent. Being Rumford, he
started several projects at once, putting out feelers
both in England and America for a situation that
would be both financially and politically advantageous. His maneuvering in the American scene is
one of the almost incredible incidents of his far
from commonplace life.

Count Rumford turned his thoughts toward retiring to his native land either as a soldier or as a
country gentleman. He wrote to his childhood

friend, Loammi Baldwin, in Woburn, Massachusetts: "From forty to one hundred acres of good
land with wood and water belonging to it, if possible in a retired situation, from one to four miles
from Cambridge, with or without a neat comfortable house upon it, would satisfy all my wishes. . . .
I would want nothing from the land but pleasure
grounds and grass for my cows and horses and extensive kitchen garden and fruit garden. I would
wish much for a few acres of wood and also for a
stream of fresh water or a large pond or the neigh-
borhood of one, for without shady trees and water
there can be no rural beauty."

Romantic as this picture may seem, it is doubtful
that Rumford had any real intention of settling back
to the agrarian life of a country squire. This idyllic
setting could be a respectable retreat if necessary,
and probably was intended to supply atmosphere,
and to provide a conspicuous though dignified
background from which he could pursue any of the
several ambitious schemes he had in mind to keep
himself in the public eye.

Rumford counted as one of his good friends the
Honorable Rufus King, who was at that time American Ambassador to Britain. A letter which King
wrote at Rumford's request to the American Secretary of State revealed the direction his thoughts
were taking. "He proposes to establish himself at or
near Cambridge, to live there in the Character of a
German count. . . . His knowledge, particularly in
the military department, may be of great use to
us. The Count is well acquainted with, and has had
much experience in, the establishment of cannon
foundries. That which he established in Bavaria is
spoken of in very high terms, as well as certain
improvements he has introduced in the mounting

of flying artillery. He possesses an extensive military library and assures me that he wishes nothing more than to be useful to our country. . . . I am persuaded that his principles are good and his talents and information uncommonly extensive. From the inquiry which I have made on this head, I am convinced that his political sentiments are correct. Be good enough to communicate this letter to the President."

Proposal to Establish a U.S. Military Academy

During the next three months, Rumford's nebulous ideas of settling in America had crystallized into a definite plan—that of the establishment of an American military academy. This concept was enthusiastically endorsed by Rufus King, who sent Rumford's proposal to James McHenry, the American Secretary of War. Secretary McHenry in turn passed the suggestion on to the President. President John Adams was duly sympathetic to the idea, but commented, "You know the difficulties those gentlemen who have left the country as he did, either to give or receive entire satisfaction. I should not scruple, however, to give him any of the appointments you mention, and to leave it with you to make such proposals to him through Mr. King . . . as you should think fit." This was June 24, 1799.

In those days there was no efficient federal investigating agency. Not until some months later did official Washington awake to the realization that the man they were considering as the first superintendent of the military academy at West Point had been, in fact, a spy for the enemy during the Revolution. It is interesting to read the communications that went back and forth, particularly between Mr. King and the Count, when the United States government decided to unhook itself from any alliance with Count Rumford, whose primary desire was to remain in an honorable light in the public eye. An arrangement was finally arrived at, and King wrote back to his government, "I have duly received your letter . . . respecting Count Rumford. We had some conversation upon the subject which will resume. I, however, conclude from what has already passed, that though much gratified by the offer, he will wisely decline accepting it."

Rufus King and Rumford remained good friends throughout all this time, and King did everything in his power to make Rumford's exit as graceful as possible. After having received assurances privately that all offers from the United States government would be "wisely declined," King wrote an official invitation: "In the course of the last year, we have made provisions for the institution of a military academy, and we wish to commit its formation to your experience and its future government to your care. . . . In addition to the superintendence of the military academy, I am authorized to offer to you the appointment of Inspector General of the Artillery of the United States."

Rumford Declines

Count Rumford's carefully worded answer was submitted to Mr. King privately for editing and comment. He replied formally and at length to "His Excellency, Rufus King, Envoy extraordinary and Minister plenipotentiary to the United States at the Court of London. . . . Engagements which great obligations have rendered sacred and inviolable put it out of my power to dispose of my time and services with that unreserved freedom which would be necessary in order to enable me to accept of those generous offers which the Executive Government of the United States has been pleased to propose to me."

What were these "engagements which great obligations have rendered sacred and inviolable"? As we shall see, they took the Count into new fields but followed a now familiar pattern, in which proposals for the public weal always seemed to result in private promotion.

CHAPTER 15

The Royal Institution of Great Britain

Count Rumford had spent a great deal of time writing up his essays and trying to get before the world his ideas on stoves, cooking utensils, lamps, and the many other utilitarian devices based on his physical theories. He was disappointed in the response to his writings. Few of the artisans and workmen who would be building his devices saw his essays; most of them could not even read. To solve this problem, the Count began to develop the concept of a museum of science. Some of his other schemes in England having failed, he decided to embark on a full-scale project which turned out to be the first museum of science for the instruction of the general public on the improvement of practical devices in the scientific world.

The plan was set in motion by the circulation of a set of proposals written by Count Rumford to those patrons of science and others in high places who might be disposed to subscribe fifty guineas toward the establishment of this institute: "The proposals for forming by subscription in the metropolis of the British Empire, a public institution for diffusing the knowledge and facilitating the general introduction of useful mechanical inventions and improvements, and for teaching by courses of philosophical lectures and experiments, the applications of science, to the common purposes of life." The proposals offered a complete and detailed description of what the institution should be and how it should be run. It was Rumford from beginning to end. With the supreme confidence of the complete egotist, Rumford set up the institution to diffuse knowledge and introduce useful mechanical inventions he himself had worked on—but to the almost complete exclusion of any branch of science in which he had not interested himself.

A list of the mechanical inventions to be exhibited illustrates how completely this was to be the Rumford institution.

Cottage fireplaces and kitchen utensils for cottages.

A complete kitchen for a farmhouse with all the necessary utensils.

A complete kitchen with kitchen utensils for the family of a gentleman of fortune.

A complete laundry for a gentleman's family or for a public hospital, including boilers, washing rooms, ironing rooms, drying rooms, etc.

Several of the most improved German, Swedish, and Russian stoves for heating rooms and passages.

Open chimney fireplaces on the most approved principles.

Ornamental, as well as economical, grates for chimney fireplaces.

Ornamental stoves in the form of elegant chimney pieces for halls, drawing rooms, eating rooms, etc.

Brewers' boilers with improved fireplaces.

Distillers' coppers with improved fireplaces and improved condensers.

Large boilers for kitchens of hospitals and ships' coppers with improved fireplaces.

You may recognize in the foregoing a reflection of

the Count's published papers on mechanical contrivances. Nor were the more theoretical of his published papers neglected, since one of the functions of his institution was to provide public lectures on scientific subjects. The lecture topics were to include:

Heat and its application to the various purposes of life.

Combustion of inflammable bodies and the relative quantities of heat produced by the different substances used as fuel.

The management of fire and economy of fuel.

Principles of the warmth of clothing.

The effect of heat and of cold, and of hot and of cold winds on the human body in sickness and in health.

The effect of breathing vitiated and confined air.

The means that may be used to render dwelling houses comfortable and salubrious.

The nature of those changes that are produced on substances used as a food in the various processes of cookery.

Here again, we find a list of those scientific subjects about which Rumford himself had written, and we cannot escape the feeling that the Count was setting up his own scientific monument. He was not very subtle about it either, because in a letter to Loammi Baldwin he wrote, "The success of the undertaking will be productive of . . . much good, and will place me in a distinguished situation in the eyes of the world and of posterity."

Public Support of Rumford's Plan

The public response to Rumford's enterprise was very encouraging to all concerned. Fifty-eight proprietors willing to contribute fifty guineas were found. A house on Albemarle Street in London was bought, and the necessary extensive modifications were started. A Glasgow physician, Dr. Thomas Garnett, was engaged as a professor of natural philosophy and chemistry to give a series of public lectures. A young architect was appointed clerk to the treasurer, secretary, clerk of the works, and entrusted with the responsibility of forming an industrial school for mechanics. Thus was formed the Royal Institution of Great Britain.

In 1800, a new and very long prospectus was written by Count Rumford. A large number of copies were printed and given the widest possible circulation, not only in England, but elsewhere in Europe and America as well. Dr. Garnett was giving a popular series of lectures, a new theater was being built, large committees for scientific investigation were being formed, and it seemed as if the institute were on its way to success. Below the surface, however, all was not well. The seeds of internal strife which Rumford was sowing can be imagined from a letter the Count wrote to Professor Pictet in Geneva, in July of that year. "The arduous and important undertaking in which I am engaged in this metropolis . . . has met with universal approbation and liberal support. . . . The approbation of foreigners of distinction is a great support and assistance to me and facilitates my labors by silencing and keeping in awe those who might wish to oppose me. . . . Hitherto, my exertions have been completely successful. My competitors and opponents have been defeated and all my plans have been adopted without any alterations."

Rumford's dictatorial personality was breeding trouble for his institute. A diarist of note, Joseph

Farrington, wrote in his journal, "Count Rumford had made himself very disagreeable by his violent, overbearing manners." About this time there appeared in public print, under the name of Peter Pindar, an epistle to Count Rumford, containing these lines:

> But what an insolence in me to prate,
> Pretend to him to open wisdom's gate,
> Who spurns advice like weeds where'r it springs,
> Disdaining counsel, though it comes from kings.

"Here I must beg leave to differ from the Count. Although a man may, like the Count, possess *extraordinary intellect*, and though a man may be the *best judge* of *himself*, nevertheless, it is *indecorous* to treat the opinions of *others* with contempt. The Count's constant assertion is, 'I never was yet in the wrong. I know everything.' Granting this to be true, the declaration, nevertheless, is *arrogant* and supercilious."

Rumford expressed a missionary zeal in his "great and most important undertaking, an attempt to turn the attention of a wealthy, luxurious, and idle nobility to the amusement of scientific pursuits and the pleasure of doing good, to counteract the evils which result from riches and excessive indulgence, and to retard and prolong the fall of a great nation which has passed the zenith of human glory!"

The society at which all this reformation was aimed did not take Rumford's endeavors very seriously. As Elizabeth Lady Holland wrote in her journal for March 19, 1800: "This institution of Rumford's furnishes ridiculous stories. The other day they tried the effect of the gas so poetically described by Beddoes; it exhilarates the spirits, distends the vessels, and in short, gives life to the whole machine. The first subject was a corpulent middle-aged gentleman who, after inhaling a sufficient dose, was requested to describe to the company his sensation. 'Why, I only feel stupid.' This intelligence was received amid a burst of applause, most probably not for the novelty of the information. Sir Coxe Hippisley was the next who submitted to the operation, but the *effect* upon him was so *animating* that the ladies tittered, held up their hands, and declared themselves satisfied." This particular lecture at the Royal Institution was so worthy of note that the caricaturist James Gillray immortalized a similar scene, reproduced in Plate VII.

The Arrival of Young Humphry Davy

Dr. Garnett had never impressed Rumford, and at the close of his lecture series for 1801, Garnett was asked to resign. In his place, the Count appointed Humphry Davy, whose subsequent tremendous scientific accomplishments were to keep the Royal Institution alive as a power in the scientific life of Great Britain.

Humphry Davy was then an uncultured country youth of twenty-two, employed in Dr. Beddoes' Medical Pneumatic Institution at Bristol. The Pneumatic Institution "was established for the purpose of investigating the medical powers of facetious airs of gases," which were considerably popular with the faddists of that day. Two years earlier, Davy had published in the West County Contributions a paper entitled "On Heat, Light, and the Combination of Light." Presumably, it was this long anti-caloric paper that was responsible for the notice which Rumford took of Davy. This experiment of Davy's is often coupled with Rumford's in physics textbooks, as leading to the downfall of the caloric theory.

Humphry Davy, even to this day, is one of the most famous scientists Britain has produced. The fact that Rumford found him at an obscure laboratory and brought him into prominence by making him a lecturer at the Royal Institution will forever be to Rumford's credit. However, it was almost a comedy of misconceptions that brought these two men together and continues to link their anticaloric experiments with the historical development of our theories of heat. We mentioned before that Rumford is often credited by modern writers with having "annihilated the material theory of heat," and with being the father of our modern concepts that heat is a form of energy. We saw that this is interpretation far from historical fact. Rumford's tremendous political, scientific, and social reputation was largely responsible for landing this credit at his doorstep. Almost parallel was the contribution of Humphry Davy, whose scientific reputation was so great that his work is often cited as being equally decisive and sometimes even superior to Rumford's in scientific value. The historical facts do not bear this assessment out. In fact, Davy indulged in speculations of the wildest nature, about which he was very sensitive in later life, and exposure of his rashness may serve as a stern warning to those who would quote scientific history without proper regard for the historical facts. It is sometimes written that Davy furthered Rumford's fight against the caloric theory by showing that "ice could be melted by friction in an evacuated bell jar by rubbing two pieces together by clockwork." The

quotation marks are important since they are copied
from a current physics textbook. Actually, he did
not melt ice by friction in an evacuated bell jar,
but in the open air. He did carry on an experiment
in an evacuated bell jar, rubbing two pieces of
beeswax together, and in his attempt to show that
light is not an effect of heat, he proved experimen-
tally that particles of iron could be heated to the
melting point without giving out any light.

It might be worthwhile spending a little time
looking into the details of Davy's original experiment. Davy says that he wired two pieces of ice
to two iron bars and that "by a peculiar mechanism" the ice was kept in violent friction for some
minutes. The pieces of ice "were almost entirely
converted into water." The water was found to be
at 35° "after remaining in an atmosphere at a lower
temperature for some minutes." The whole experiment was fantastic as described, and undoubtedly
the ice was melted by conduction through the iron
bars which held the ice pieces together. The ama-
teurish aspect of this experiment should in no way
detract from the greatness of Humphry Davy as a
scientist when he became trained, but as an un-
tutored lad of nineteen he apparently did not understand the concept of scientific experimentation,
and his association with Rumford, as a result of his
ill-conceived experiments, thereby seems all the
more remarkable.

On May 25, 1801, Rumford gave the managers
of the Royal Institution his report on progress,
which was a picture of the Institution as he had
labored night and day for three years to make it
and as he wished it to be. He dismissed the profes-
sors, the lecturers, and the lecture room with four
lines, and then went on to discuss at great length

the laboratory for carrying on the processes of practical chemistry, the workshops "where models of new and useful inventions will be constructed." He told of the workmen already engaged—"a mathematical instrument maker, a model maker, a cabinet maker, a carpenter, a worker in brass and copper, a tin plate worker, and an iron plate worker. To these will be soon added: bricklayers and stonemasons, who will instruct and enable to instruct others in setting new invented grates, roasters, ovens, broilers, etc." He described the complete kitchen, the printing office, the reading room, the repository for models, and the advance plans for various trade schools for the purpose of "diffusing the knowledge and facilitating the general introduction of useful mechanical inventions and improvements."

In three years, Rumford had created an industrial school for mechanics, a society for diffusing useful knowledge by publications and lectures, a mechanical exhibition of things useful to the poor and to the rich, an association for the promotion of scientific investigations by means of different committees of workers, and a convenient club with a school of cookery attached, and all this under the Royal Institution. Under a single roof was the "Rumford Institution," created by the dictatorial authority of its founder, but the same ruthless energy that had established the Institution began to threaten its very life. Such grandiose and comprehensive plans could not be maintained without great expense, and the "institution borne by public subscription" had to have solid and continuing support of the "wealthy, luxurious, and idle nobility" which Count Rumford treats with such scorn in his letters. London society did not take kindly to his attitude, and the Institution's income fell from over eleven thousand

pounds in 1800 to less than thirty-five hundred
pounds in 1801, at a time when workers were being hired, and facilities expanded, and expenditures
increasing. In all fairness to Count Rumford, it
must be stated that his personality was by no means
the only cause of the difficulty in which the Royal
Institution found itself. He wanted the Institution
to be a place for public display of the latest improvements in mechanical devices. As he tried to
collect such devices, he ran into real trouble with
the inventors who hoped to earn a proper recompense for their latest improvement. The inventors
were quite rightly opposed to publicizing their se-
crets or in any way weakening their patents. Most
powerful among the voices raised in protest at this
policy of the Royal Institution was that of James
Watt.

James Watt Protests

In the public mind, Watt's name is forever linked
to the steam engine, but it is even more familiar to
physics students because our unit of power is named
in his honor. He was a Scottish instrument maker
who learned his basic science at the University of
Edinburgh, and spent his life designing, redesign-
ing, and improving a practical steam engine, in
partnership with a businessman, Matthew Boulton.
From the time of the American Revolution until
1800, the company of Boulton & Watt had a monopoly on steam engines, their improvement and
design, and the idea of letting Rumford exhibit
models of their machines at the Royal Institution
worried them so that they tried to take legal action
against the Count to prevent establishment of the
museum. If you think about the reason for such ex-

aggerated alarm, you will find the timing particularly interesting. The Watt-Boulton basic patents, which they had obtained from Parliament in 1775, ran out in 1800, and Watt and Boulton became singularly sensitive to any move that might weaken their extremely profitable monopoly or even remotely threaten it. From their plant in Birmingham many letters were written to influential Londoners in an effort to undermine Rumford and the Royal Institution itself. This kind of pressure accounts, at least in part, for the emphasis on Rumford's own inventions at the Royal Institution, where no patent or legal complication had to be considered.

As the financial condition of the Royal Institution deteriorated and the clamor for Rumford to change his concept of the Institution and to soften his despotic behavior became more insistent, the Count began to lose his enthusiasm. All during the time the Royal Institution was being set up, Count Rumford was still in the pay of the Bavarian government. As soon as it appeared that the Institution was a brilliant international success, pressure was brought to bear on him to return to Munich and establish something similar there. The Elector Karl Theodor had died in 1799, leaving his throne to his nephew, the Duc de Deux-Ponts, the same man who had originally persuaded Rumford to enter the Bavarian service. Rumford had not been to Bavaria since the new Elector, Maximilian Joseph, had taken power, but in September 1801, he left London to pay his respects to the Court of Munich.

Return to the Continent

From Munich, on October 2nd, Rumford wrote, "I arrived here late last evening and early this morning went to pay my respects to the Elector, who received me with all imaginable kindness. He appears to have plenty of business for me in an academy he is about building. But, as things are not yet in readiness to begin, I am excused from remaining. Instead of which, I return to England to put an end to the work begun there—that of the Royal Institution. I owe so much to the Elector, it is my duty to do all in my power to give him satisfaction. Beside, he says I should be President of the academy when done."

Rumford stayed in Munich less than two weeks and then departed for England by way of Paris, where he had some business of the Elector's to attend to. He hoped to spend not more than eight to ten days in the French capital before returning to his responsibilities in London. His reckoning had not taken Parisian hospitality into account, however, or the sharp contrast in attitude he found in the two cities. In London he was beginning to encounter hostility, apathy, and criticism from scientists and ridicule from society. In Paris he was greeted with tremendous respect, was feted by Napoleon, honored by Talleyrand, and lionized by members of the French Academy of Sciences. His name was placed on the list of foreign associates of the Academy, following that of Thomas Jefferson, President of the United States. Furthermore, he found himself much sought after by one of the richest and most fashionable ladies of Paris—Madame Lavoisier, widow of the famous French chemist. It is not at all surprising that his short stay lengthened to seven weeks before he could tear himself away.

The London to which he returned had become no more hospitable in his absence, and the lure of

Paris and Munich proved irresistible. The next five months in London were occupied mostly in putting his personal business in order and trying to assure himself that the Royal Institution would not disintegrate without his guiding hands. His final report to the managers of the Institution concludes, "The Royal Institution of Great Britain may . . . be considered as finished and freely established. That it may long continue to flourish is, no doubt, the ardent wish of those who are connected with it, and also of all those who are acquainted with the principles on which it is founded and who know how powerfully it must contribute to the general diffusion of an active spirit of inquiry and useful improvements among all ranks of society." With this happy, final statement, Rumford considered his mission completed, his achievement secure. He methodically catalogued all his belongings in his house in London and left England, never to return.

CHAPTER 16

The Courtship of Madame Lavoisier

Count Rumford had promised the Elector of Bavaria that he would return to set up an academy
of arts and sciences in Munich. After he left London he again spent a few weeks in Paris, as much
in the company of Madame Lavoisier as he could,
and then continued on to Munich to make himself
useful to Maximilian Joseph. His heart, however,
was not really in his Munich assignment, and he
tried desperately to be released from his duties in
Bavaria so that he might spend his time with his
new friend in the French capital. But in spite of
Rumford's recent friendship with Napoleon, the
suspicious First Consul was not taking any chances
with British spies at a time when he was threaten-
ing invasion of the British Isles. And it must be
remembered that Count Rumford still held the rank
of colonel in the British Army. Try as he would,
Count Rumford could not get permission to enter
France. The next best thing was to get Madame
Lavoisier to visit him.

In the summer of 1803, Rumford took Madame
Lavoisier on an extended tour of Bavaria and
Switzerland. Apparently they both had a wonder-
ful time, despite the fact that she did not really like
travel and was something less than fascinated by his
constant talk of physics and the experiments that

occupied his days, even amid the grandeur of the
Swiss Alps. One of these experiments, which he
carried out while they were staying in a chalet over-
looking the Mer de Glace, above Chamonix, was
a follow-up to his previous studies of the maximum
density of water. He describes these experiments
vividly:

At the surface of a solid mass of ice of vast
thickness and extent, we discovered a pit perfectly
cylindrical, about seven inches in diameter and
more than four feet deep, quite full of water. On
examining it on the inside with a pole, I found that
its sides were polished and that its bottom was
hemispherical and well defined. This pit was not
quite perpendicular to the plane of the horizon but
inclined a little toward the south as it descended,
and in consequence of this inclination, its mouth,
or opening at the surface of the ice, was not circular but elliptical.

From our guides we learned that these cylindrical holes are frequently found on the level parts of
the ice, that they are formed during the summer
increasing gradually in depth as long as the hot
weather continues, but that they are frozen up and
disappear on the return of winter. . . . From
whence comes the heat that melts the ice continually at the bottom of the pit and how does it happen that this heat acts on the *bottom* of the pit only
and not on its sides?

These curious phenomena may, I think, be explained in the following manner. The warm winds
which in summer blow over the surface of this
column of ice-cold water must undoubtedly communicate some small degree of heat to those particles of the fluid with which this warm air comes
into immediate contact. And the particles of water
at the surface so heated, being rendered specifically
heavier than they were before by this small in-

1

crease of temperature, sink slowly to the bottom of
the pit where they come into contact with the ice
and communicate to it the heat by which the depth
of the pit is continually increased.

Count Rumford then complains rather bitterly
about other natural philosophers who did not accept his theories that heat was transmitted in a
liquid by means of its convection currents, and that
water goes through a maximum density point at
41° F. He says, "I wish that gentlemen who refuse
their assent to the opinions I have advanced respecting the causes of this curious phenomenon
would give a better explanation of it than that
which I have ventured to offer. I could likewise
wish that they would inform us how it happens that
the water at the bottom of all deep lakes remains
constantly at the same temperature, and above all,
how the cylindrical pits above described are formed
in the immense masses of solid and compact ice
which compose the glaciers of Chamonix."

Madame Lavoisier was a woman of great social
power and prestige, and it did not take her long
after she returned to Paris to persuade the government to allow Count Rumford to enter the French
capital. By early spring of 1804, he had settled in
Paris and finally bought a house for himself and
Madame on the Rue d'Anjou, close to the Tuileries
Gardens and the Champs-Elysées. He looked on
this new house as a second and personal Royal Institution, and set himself busily to the task of re-
building the interior with all his most recent improvements.

It was not until after the detailed paperwork of
transferring Madame Lavoisier's considerable fortune to the Count was under way that he discovered that if he were actually to marry Madame

Lavoisier, he would need some legal documents with regard to his own freedom. Sarah Walker Thompson had died on January 19, 1792, but he needed legally valid answers to such questions as when and where. Urgent letters to Woburn, Massachusetts, and Concord, New Hampshire, were sent off, with apparently some annoyance on Rumford's part that such details had to bother him. France was in the middle of an expansionist war, and all her neighbors were armed against her. Communication by letter was precarious in those days anyway, and with the added hazards of war, it is not astonishing that it took until the autumn of 1805 to get all the necessary information that would allow him to wed the former Madame Lavoisier.

During this period he was far from idle. He spent some of his time in Munich directing the Elector's Academy of Arts and Sciences, but most of it in Paris improving the house in the Rue d'Anjou and carrying on detailed experiments which earned him a reputation as a "grave philosopher" in the eyes of the French Academy. About his improvements to his house, Rumford wrote, in his modest way, "I have the best founded hope of passing my days in peace and quiet in this paradise of a place, made what it is by me—my money, skill, and direction. In short, it is all but a paradise."

CHAPTER 17

Disharmony: Legal and Marital

On the 24th of October, 1805, Madame Lavoisier and Count Rumford finally were married. It was a fashionable match, and greetings from nobility poured into their villa. With a sly dig, a London newspaper reported, "Married: In Paris, Count Rumford to the widow of Lavoisier; by which nuptial experiment he obtains a fortune of 8,000 pounds per annum—the most effective of all the Rumfordizing projects for keeping a house warm."

If the Count had a strong personality, so did Madame. And in keeping with the fame of the name of Lavoisier, she insisted that her legal name should be Madame Lavoisier de Rumford. If this hurt the Count's pride, he did not complain about it, but wrote, "I flatter myself I am settled down here for life, far removed from wars and all arduous duties, as a recompense for past services with plenty to live upon and at liberty to pursue my own natural propensities such as have occupied me through life—a life, as I try to fancy, that may come under the denomination of a benefit to mankind."

Rumford Designs a Lamp

There is no doubt that Rumford looked forward to spending the rest of his life as a wealthy gentleman of leisure, busily occupied in doing experiments in physics and applying his knowledge to improvements in the technology of light and heat. One of his main interests in his semi-retirement in Paris was furthering the improvements he had started in Munich for creating better lamps, now not for his military workhouses but for the use of society in general. His first published work on the design of lamps was read before the National Institute of France on the 20th of March, 1806. Despite the unquestionable superiority of the Argand burner, which he had used in his houses of industry in Bavaria, these lamps had one serious flaw. The oil reservoir was directly below the wick, and the viscosity of the commonly used whale and colza oils was so great that, as the lamp burned, it became more and more difficult for the oil to rise in the wick, the light growing weaker and weaker. In his paper before the Academy of Sciences, he described a type of construction that maintained the oil height on the wick by feeding the burner from a circular reservoir in the form of a hollow ring surrounding the burner and at the same height as the burner. In the Argand lamp, which depended for its brightness on the free flow of air in the immediate vicinity of the flame, the air was drawn up along the axis of a hollow wick. To get this air flowing around the wick, the lamps were customarily suspended from above, so that the mounting on the base would not interfere with air flow. Rumford worked very hard at various designs permitting free air flow without making it impossible to adjust the height of the wick, even on a table lamp. He succeeded by putting ventilating holes near the base of the lamp. His own figure of his successful construction is illustrated in Fig. 12. (A photograph of an existing Rumford lamp is shown in Plate VIII.)

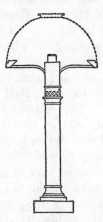

FIG. 12. Rumford's table illuminator.

Involved in a Lawsuit

Rumford was always proud of the fact that he never patented any of his inventions. He preferred the role of selfless benefactor of scientific progress, offering to others freely the ideas and opportunities for further development which his own experimental genius might stimulate. All was not smooth sailing, however, and litigation arose over some of his lamps. The story of the lawsuit in which Rumford became embroiled suggests strongly that his motives were not as disinterested as he would have had the world believe.

Rumford first announced his improvements on the Argand burner before the Academy, in March 1806. A description was published in the May issue of *Nicholson's Journal* of that year and in the *Mem-*

oirs of the French Institute in 1807. Since he frowned on patents, for himself at least, these improvements must have seemed available for manufacture by anyone. However, Rumford had a particular lampmaker by the name of Jerome Parquet, who sued a relative of Argand, who was at that time making lamps under a French patent. Parquet claimed that the Argand patent was invalid since Rumford had publicly described his inventions some years earlier. This relative of Argand, who was his successor, was a man named Bordier. Bordier countered with the reply that a year before Argand died, in 1803, he had submitted a description of his lamps to the French government, but that because they were difficult to construct, he had abandoned this design. In 1804, Bordier proposed the same lamp to the administration of a theater in Lyon, and gave a public demonstration of the device in May of that year. Monsieur Parquet, Rumford's lampmaker, testified that it was late in the year 1805, that the Count had for the first time instructed him to build one of the lamps shown in Fig. 12. In May of 1806, Bordier submitted his lamp for evaluation by the French Academy, and five commissioners were named, one of whom was Rumford himself. To quote from the lawyer's brief in the patent case: "In their report . . . the commissioners gave an account . . . not only of all the characteristics of the lamps, but also of all the experiments which had a more or less remote bearing on . . . the instruments. In this report, written with great care, there was no issue of Rumford's priority. If the last-named gentleman had been the sole commissioner, one might think that he might have shown, on this occasion, either an excess of modesty or an excess of generosity. But his four colleagues would not have allowed him to be despoiled in this matter for the benefit of a plagiarist."

Quite apart from the question of the original invention, Monsieur Thilorier, Bordier's lawyer, also tried to prove that Rumford was guilty of criminal intent to incite others to transgress French law. He based his charges on the quotation from one of Rumford's essays. "Monsieur de Rumford, who does not believe in patents and who regards most people as pirates made rich at his expense, concludes his work with the following reflection. 'I desire only that the whole world should profit by it without preventing others from using it with equal freedom.' A foreigner, whom France has heaped with honors, dares to invite the artisans of France to violate the laws of their land. . . . 'You may (he tells them in so many words) manufacture the objects described in Bordier's patent . . . and if the patentee dares to invoke against you a law of which I disapprove . . . maintain that it is I who am the inventor of the lamps. My name is sufficient to make him tremble and the little note in my great discourse is for you the head of Medusa!'"

That no love was lost between the lawyer and the Count can be readily recognized from the following statement read into the court record by Monsieur Thilorier. "I visited Rumford at his house so that he would know what was taking place. Nothing was roused but his anger. Our words of peace were squandered. . . . This very haughty and very uncivil nobleman, who received us on our feet and in his antechamber, who dared to tell us that we were knowingly defending an infamous case . . . concluded by saying that 'he will write to the Emperor and if Bordier does not forfeit his patent, Count Rumford will leave

France!'" To which Monsieur Thilorier commented, "It would be without doubt a calamity for France to lose a man such as Rumford. But if to keep him it is necessary to abolish a law favorable to French industry . . . we find our regrets transformed to prayers for the departure of Monsieur de Rumford."

We do not know the exact terms of the decision in this case, but since two of Rumford's lampmakers were granted patents of improvements in the year 1813, it is obvious that Rumford won. Whether justice was done is another matter. One suspects that the pressure the Count brought to bear through his own exalted scientific reputation and through powerful friends had more to do with the result than justice did. He wrote to a friend in April of that year: "Many thanks, my very good friend, for all the trouble you have put yourself to in this business of the lamp makers who did not want to recognize my interests. I am extremely contented with the results of this affair."

The entire episode is significant, not so much for the actual judgment of the court, but for the insight it gives us into Rumford's own character. His noble pose as the benefactor of all mankind is something which he guarded jealously. Others might use ideas which he claimed as his own, but there must be no doubt in the minds of his audience as to where the credit should lie. He could never remain anonymous in his doing of good deeds.

Marital Discord

Before Rumford's marriage to Marie Lavoisier, he had said of his future wife, "She has been very handsome in her day, and even now . . . is not bad-looking." One wonders whether observations made at his dining table may account for the tone of his remarks in his essay on lamps, when he wrote, "No decayed beauty ought ever to expose her face to the direct rays of an Argand lamp . . . that mysterious light which comes from bodies moderately illuminated is certainly most favorable to female beauty and ought on that account to be preferred by all persons who are wise."

Such remarks were indications of marital trouble between Count Rumford and Madame Lavoisier. It is amazing that after having spent four to five years in each other's company, they began to have difficulties almost as soon as they were married. Writing to Woburn, on the first anniversary of his marriage, Rumford called his French wife a "female dragon," and their public display of incompatibility became common gossip in French society. Madame was fond of parties and fashionable soirées, whereas the Count longed for quiet contemplation to write and experiment.

Disagreements at the Rue d'Anjou house became quite spectacular. One of the best-known accounts tells of a peaceful afternoon when the Count, engaged in some fruitful physics experiments, was interrupted by the sounds of voices outside the villa. Putting down his apparatus, he strode angrily down to the gate to find a large party of carriages about to enter his grounds. On asking the gatekeeper what this was all about, he was told that an afternoon affair had been arranged by Madame and that these were the guests. Rumford slammed shut the great iron gates, locked them tight, put the key in his pocket, and, telling the gatekeeper under no circumstances to let anybody enter, he strode back to his laboratory. On finishing his experiment, he happened to glance out of the window in time to see Madame, with the aid of her maids, just completing the task of pouring boiling water over all his prize beds of roses.

It was obvious that two people who would go to such lengths to annoy each other were hardly capable of living together very long. Within two years of their marriage, they decided they should separate. In 1807 Count Rumford leased another villa on the edge of Paris, in Auteuil, although for one reason or another more than a year elapsed before he actually moved to his new quarters.

CHAPTER 18

Practical Science

When Count Rumford separated from Madame
Lavoisier de Rumford, he cut himself off from
most of the social life of Paris, and concentrated
his attention on his scientific work. The final phase
of his life demonstrated a remarkable scientific
productivity. Rumford became one of the active
members of the Institute, as the French Academy
of Sciences was commonly called. Not only was he
a frequent contributor to their scientific sessions
but, thanks to his experience with the Royal Institution in London, he soon found opportunity for
improving the facilities of the French Institute,
whose lighting and heating fell short of his per-
fectionism.

Lighting Improvements

One of the Count's painstaking basic investigations in connection with improvement of illumination was the separation of the diffusion of light
from its absorption. Using his photometer, he
had showed some years previously that the total
amount of light coming from a lamp was not de-
creased when a diffusing screen was placed
around the flame of the lamp. Although the illumination in any particular direction might be de-

creased, the general illumination was not, and he invented an "illuminator" in which the flame of an Argand lamp was surrounded by a spherical diffusing screen of silk. This improvement quickly appeared in the fashionable ballrooms of the times.

The auditorium of the French Institute was very badly lit by daylight, and at one of the scientific meetings Rumford made the suggestion that a great improvement would result if the clear glass of the windows was replaced by diffusing screens of ground glass. Derisive laughter greeted this suggestion, which on the surface seemed sure to make matters worse, but the jeers turned to scientific appreciation when Rumford demonstrated that his idea was eminently right.

Steam Heat

When the home of the Royal Institution in London was being fixed up, Count Rumford was able to try out, on a full operating scale, the theories which he had developed on the use of steam as a practical heating medium. The use of steam had been tried many times, but it was not until Rumford's analysis of the independent flow of the steam and the condensed water that any basic attempt had been made to understand the engineering problem. Rumford's studies showed that a clear path must be provided for the travel of the steam into the top of a radiator and the condensed water out of the bottom. In completing the design of the heating system for the Royal Institution, the Count invented both a safety valve and an expansion section for the pipes.

A picture of his radiator construction is shown in Fig. 13, taken from one of his own papers. A

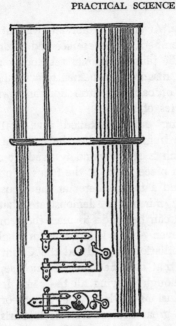

FIG. 13. Rumford's individually stoked steam radiator.

model of the complete system, showing his safety valve, the pancakelike expansion section, and a cross section of the radiator is illustrated in Plate IX.

Having demonstrated the feasibility of a complete steam-heating system in London, he naturally suggested the same for Paris. His second system not only capitalized upon his previous experience, but concentrated on the aesthetics as well. His radiators, which in London took the form of large cylindrical drums, were built into ornamental columns in Paris, giving them the air of magnificence so sought after in the European architecture of the day.

Rumford was an ardent member of the French

Academy. At times he got into violent fights with other members, but these seemed mostly to be on a scientific plane. Personal relations remained cordial. He disagreed vehemently with Lagrange on theories of capillary attraction and with Laplace on theories of heat.

Carrying out a detailed investigation of the radiation from cold bodies, he set up a demonstration which is still commonly used. It consisted of putting a piece of ice at the focus of one parabolic mirror and a thermometer at the focus of another parabolic mirror, to demonstrate that the thermometer can be made to read the temperature of the ice even across a large lecture hall. This apparent radiation of cold led the Count to the hypothesis that cold had an existence separate from heat, although obeying all the same laws. One of the conclusions he drew from this theory subjected him to a great deal of ridicule in Parisian society. If a cold body radiated "frigorific rays," as he called them, then one could stay warm in winter by wearing clothing which would reflect these frigorific rays, since the absorption of the rays obviously would cool one down. His conclusion, therefore, was that in winter one should wear shiny white clothes, which he insisted upon doing, much to the amusement of all around him.

The result of another of his experiments further stamped him as an eccentric. He was interested in the efficiency of the horse-drawn carriage, and he invented a dynamometer mounted between the drawbar and the body of a carriage to measure the force a horse needed to exert to pull a cart or carriage over roads of various construction. He then experimented with wheels of various widths and on various kinds of road surfaces, cobblestones, sand, smooth gravel, and so on, and came to the conclusion that wide wheels were much more advantageous than narrow ones on the average French roads. He had a carriage built according to his specifications and used to leave it parked in the courtyard of the Institute as a sort of museum piece. One suspects from the amount of space he used in his paper to extol the beauty of wide wheels that the carriage was definitely not elegant enough to find many enthusiasts. We also know from contemporary accounts that people used to make fun of him as he passed by.

CHAPTER 19

Last Works

Quite apart from Rumford's scientific contributions to the French Institute, his investigations in Auteuil carried forward many of his former enthusiasms. He developed a portable lamp, which came to be known as a student lamp, so popular that many examples of it exist even to this day. This lamp gave off such an intense light, relatively speaking, that one of the jokes going around French society was the story of a workman who tried to take one home to show to his family. He lit the lamp to light his way, but the brilliance of the light was so great that the poor man was blinded and wandered helplessly all night through the Bois de Boulogne.

A Drip Coffeepot

As we have seen before, Rumford believed that everything in society should be properly ordered, and anything that tended toward disorder should be studied with an eye to elimination. Intemperate use of alcohol was obviously one of the disordering forces in society, and he searched for something that would give people as much pleasure as drinking without its disorganizing effect. He came to the conclusion that coffee might be the answer, and he decided that only the difficulty of producing a

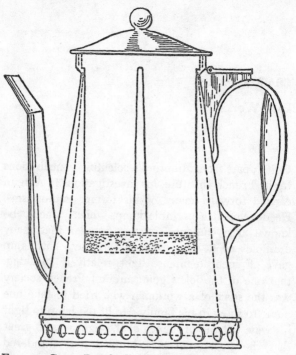

FIG. 14. Count Rumford's illustration of one of his drip coffeemakers.

good cup of coffee stood in its way to popularity. In characteristic fashion, he set about to discover what accounted for the taste of coffee. In a fairly ingenious set of experiments, he found that the taste resided in the volatile oils. How then to avoid the loss of these necessary oils? He was sure that they would be lost in a boiling process, and from his previous studies on the motion of current in liquids came two conclusions: (1) that the coffee must be made at a constant temperature, and (2) that it must be made in a sealed container. His solution was to invent what we now call a drip

coffeemaker, surrounded by a water jacket to keep
the whole mass of coffee at a constant temperature.
A picture of his completed coffee machine is shown
in Fig. 14. There still exist some detailed drawings
of the Count's attempt to make a portable coffeemaker for the traveler's convenience and pleasure.
Whether Rumford actually made such a device we
do not know, but the pictures of Plate X show a
portable coffeemaker constructed from his manuscript drawings.

To illustrate the range of problems he worked on
in his Auteuil laboratory, the following partial list
of papers he published in these last few years is of
interest:

"New Experiments and Observations on the Propagation of Heat in Liquids"

"Note on the Use of Steam as a Source of Heat in
the Distillation of Brandy"

"Experiments and Observations on the Internal
Adhesion of Molecules of Water"

"Description of a New Boiler Constructed with a
View to the Saving of Fuel"

"Notice of an Experiment on the Use of the Heat
of Steam in Place of That of an Open Fire in the
Making of Soap"

"Continuation of Experiments and Observations on
the Internal Adhesion of Molecules of Water"

"Study of the Progress of the Slow Spontaneous
Mixing of Certain Liquids Amongst Themselves"

"Experiments and Observations on the Cooling of
Liquids in Gilded and Ungilded Porcelain Vases"

"Observations on the Proper Method to be Employed for Heating the Auditorium of the Institute
of France"

"Experiments and Observations on the Advantage
of Using Wheels with Wide Felloes for Carts and
Carriages"

"On the Management of Light in Illumination with an Account of a New Portable Lamp"

"Account of Some New Experiments on Wood and Charcoal"

"An Inquiry Concerning the Source of the Light Which is Manifested in the Combustion of Inflammable Bodies"

"Inquiries Concerning the Heat Developed in Combustion with a Description of a New Calorimeter"

"Research on the Heat Developed in Combustion"

"On the Quantities of Heat Developed in the Condensation of Vapors of Water and in That of Alcohol"

"On the Capacity of Heat or Calorific Power of Various Liquids"

"Inquiries Relative to the Structure of Wood: The Specific Gravity of Its Solid Parts and the Quantity of Liquids and Elastic Fluids Contained in It Under Various Circumstances, the Quantity of Charcoal to be Obtained from It, and the Quantity of Heat Produced by Its Combustion"

"On the Salubrity of Warm Rooms"

"On the Salubrity of Warm Bathing"

"On the Use of Steam as a Vehicle for Transporting Heat"

"On the Management of Light"

"On the Source of Light in Combustion"

"Of the Excellent Qualities of Coffee and the Art of Making It in the Highest Perfection"

There are many records of visitors who came to him to talk about science, engineering, and sociology. To illustrate the effort which some of these people made to discuss some of their problems with him, we note that at a time when all communication between England and France was cut off by war between the two nations, the French Emperor himself gave permission to Sir Humphry Davy to visit his old sponsor. Davy brought his young assistant to meet the Count, a lad by the name of Michael Faraday.

Cuvier's Eulogy

Count Rumford died very suddenly in August 1814, but he had planned for death with the same combination of orderliness and dramatic imagination that characterized most of his life. He had drawn up a very interesting will leaving the residue of his estate to Harvard College, and, as if to guarantee that his wishes would be acceptable on the American scene which he had abandoned so early, he had asked the French hero of the American Revolution, the Marquis de Lafayette, to sign the will as a witness. Rumford was buried in a small cemetery in Auteuil. His grave is cared for by Harvard University, in honor of the man who endowed the natural-philosophy professorship that bears his name.

Rumford's stormy life and brilliant but difficult temperament were eulogized with due ceremony, according to the custom of the French Academy, by Baron Cuvier, the naturalist and Academy secretary, whose comments summarized quite frankly the contemporary feeling. Cuvier said in part, "Nothing would have been wanting to his happiness had the amenity of his behavior equalled his ardor for public utility. But it must be acknowledged that he manifested in his conversation and in his whole conduct a feeling which must appear very extraordinary in a man so uniformly well-treated by others and who had himself done so much good. It was without loving or esteeming his fellow creatures that he had done them all these services. Apparently, the vile passions which he had observed in the wretches committed to his care or those other passions which his good fortune had excited among his rivals had soured him against human nature. Nor did he think that the care of their own welfare ought to be confided to men in common. That desire, which seems to them so natural, of examining how they are ruled, was in his eyes but a facetious product of false knowledge. He considered the Chinese government as the nearest to perfection, because in delivering up the people to the absolute power of men of knowledge alone, and in raising each of these in the hierarchy according to the degree of his knowledge, it made in some measures so many millions of hands the passive organs of the will of a few good heads. An empire such as he conceived would not have been more difficult for him to manage than his barracks and poorhouses. For this he trusted especially to the power of order. He called order the necessary auxiliary of genius, the only possible instrument of real good, and almost a subordinate divinity regulating this lower world. He himself in his person was in all imaginable points a model of order. His wants, his labors, and his pleasures were calculated like his experiments. In short, he permitted himself nothing superfluous, not even a step or a word, and it was in the strictest sense that he took the word *superfluous*. This was, no doubt, a sure means of devoting his whole strength to useful pursuits, but it could not make him an agreeable being in the society of his fellows. The world requires a little more freedom and is so constituted that a certain height of perfection often appears to it a defect, when the person does not take as much pains to conceal his knowledge as he has taken to acquire it."

Conclusion

One large and puzzling question remains about Count Rumford. Why is it that so few people today have ever heard of him? Here was a man of real scientific imagination and persistence, who developed a number of important theories from careful observations, a physicist who championed our modern research method of studying fundamentals before trying to make practical applications. He himself initiated many of our modern improvements in day-to-day living. As a sociologist, he initiated extremely advanced experiments in organizing people to understand and make use of new information. Yet he is almost unknown today.

There is, of course, no simple answer to the question, but there is a lesson to be learned in searching for the answer. Throughout this book you must have been struck by the fact that Thompson's attitude toward people was not one that endeared him to those around him. He was not really interested in people and their human problems. He tried to use people rather than to help them. He never seemed able to enjoy the fruits of his labors, because the means that he used in obtaining many of his ends appeared neither honorable nor justifiable.

Physics is not divorced from the morals of society,

and a physicist who violates the standards of men about him cuts himself off from rewards which might be his if he showed a normal respect for human values. There is nothing about being a scientist, an engineer, or a sociologist that excuses amoral behavior, and the result of Rumford's antisocial attitudes was to cut him off from the very fame he sought. People who tried to live and to work with him found it so difficult to give him credit for his real achievements that when his life was over they just forgot him as fast as possible.

In digging out the facts of history, we find that Rumford's scientific and technological contributions loom very large. We can learn a great deal of the methodology of physics and engineering by a study of his work. A more important lesson even than this, however, is to learn from the story of his life that the really lasting impression a man may make on history depends as much on his contributions to society in terms of his own character and values as it does on the magnitude of his purely scientific achievements.

Appendix

The coded part of the letter reproduced on page 42 has been deciphered to read as follows:

"General Sir Benjamin Thompson is assured that he will have the whole execution of his projected reform of the military, and proposes carrying his changes through all the departments in the regiments, clothing, arms, artificers, and even in the garrisons. One of the most important parts of his plan is to increase the army, and he even proposes that it should be gradually raised to 30,000 men which he promises to effect in four years without increasing the supplies the Elector annually gives for the army expenses, which amount to 2,500,000 florins."

Bibliography

The most complete published information on Count Rumford is contained in a collection published by the American Academy of Arts and Sciences from 1870 to 1873:

"Memoir of Sir Benjamin Thompson, Count Rumford," by George E. Ellis, 680 pages.

"The Complete Works of Count Rumford"
Volume I   493 pages
Volume II   570 pages
Volume III 504 pages
Volume IV   842 pages

Unfortunately, because of their age, these volumes are relatively scarce.

Two more modern biographies have been written, drawing material from the Ellis biography although much less comprehensive in scope. These are:

"Count Rumford of Massachusetts," by James Alden Thompson. Farrar & Rinehart, New York, 1935, 275 pages.

"An American in Europe," by Egon Larsen. Rider & Co., New York, 1953, 224 pages.

Short biographical sketches of Count Rumford

have appeared every few years since he died. Of these, two of the latest are:

"The Remarkable American Count," by E. Alexander Powell. *American Heritage*, Vol. 8, 74–77, 98–100 (1956).

"Count Rumford," by Mitchell Wilson. *Scientific American*, Vol. 203, No. 4, 158–68 (October, 1960).

Very few articles have been written specifically about Rumford's scientific work. Two papers that have recently appeared dealing with certain phases of his work are:

"Rumford's Photometer," by W. J. Sparrow. *The School Science Review*, No. 134, Nov. 1956, 43–47.

"Sir Benjamin Thompson, Count of Rumford," by C. Harrison Dwight. Privately printed 1960, 82 pages.

Most of the remaining publications on Rumford's scientific work were written by the author of this book, Sanborn C. Brown:

"The Discovery of Convection Currents by Benjamin Thompson, Count of Rumford." *American Journal of Physics*, 16, 304–5 (1948).

"Count Rumford and the Caloric Theory of Heat." *Proceedings of the American Philosophical Society*, 93, 316–25 (1949).

"The Caloric Theory of Heat." *American Journal of Physics*, 18, 367–73 (1950).

"Rumford Lamps." *Proceedings of the American Philosophical Society*, 96, 37–44 (1952).

"Count Rumford's Concept of Heat." *American Journal of Physics*, 20, 331–34 (1952).

"Count Rumford—Physicist and Technologist." *Proceedings of the American Academy of Arts and Sciences*, 82, 266–89 (1953).

"Discovery of the Differential Thermometer." *American Journal of Physics*, 22, 13–17 (1954).

"Count Rumford on Photosynthesis." *Proceedings of the American Academy of Arts and Sciences*, 86, 44–46 (1955).

"Scientific Drawings of Count Rumford at Harvard." *Harvard Library Bulletin*, 9, 350–64 (1955).

Index

"Account of Some Experiments Made to Determine the Quantities of Moisture . . . ," 52

"Account of Some Experiments Upon Gunpowder," 26

Adams, John, 123

Agriculture, Rumford and, 11–12

Alcohol, intemperate use of, 159

American Academy of Arts and Sciences, 113

American Philosophical Society, 6

American Revolution, Rumford and: as military scientist, 25–31; as officer of dragoons, 33–37; as official of British government, 23–24, 28–32; as spy, 18–22

Appleton, John, 2

Argand lamp, 79–80, 146, 154; lawsuit over, 147–50

Artillery, 122–23; cannon-boring experiments, 91–97

Baking oven, 75

Baldwin, Loammi, 4, 6–7; letters to, 11–13, 122, 129

Ballistic pendulum, 25–27

Bavaria: Academy of Arts and Sciences, 138, 141, 144; beggars and poor in, 56–62, 64, 70; gardens established, 69–71, 84; Rumford enters service of Elector, 38–46; Rumford's final visits to, 137–38, 141, 144; Rumford's rise to power in, 83–87. *See also* Karl Theodor

Bavarian Army: cannon-boring experiments with, 91–97; experiments on clothing for, 48–54; food for, 63–67, 69–70; Military Workhouse, 56–62, 64, 70, 75, 86; portable field stoves for, 116–18; reorganization of, 47–48; Rumford in command of, 114–16

Beggars, Rumford's Workhouse for, 56–62, 64, 70, 75, 86

Boerhaave's *Treatise on Fire*, 90–91

Bordier (lampmaker), 148–49

Boston, Mass., Rumford in, 3, 17, 21–22, 34

Bounty for enlisting in British Army, 35

Bradford, Mass., Rumford in, 8, 11

British Army, Rumford and: as officer of dragoons, 33–37; as spy, 13–22; as supply official, 24, 29–31

British Foreign Office, Rumford as spy for, 39–46

British Navy, Rumford and, 26, 28–29, 31

Brown, Judge William, 22

Caloric theory of heat: Davy and, 132–34; described, 89–90, 92–93; "radiant caloric," 101; refuted in part by Rumford, 80–81, 90–106; Rumford's conception of heat, 97–99; weight of heat in, 100–2. See also Heat

Calorimeter, combustion, 72–74, 162

Cannon-boring experiments, 91–97

Capen, Hopestill, 2–3

Carnot, Sadi, 96

Carriages, horseless: experiments on, 156–57, 161

Charcoal, 162

Charleston, S.C., Rumford in, 35–36

Chimney fireplaces, 108–12

Chinese government, 164

Clothing: experiments in, 30–31, 48–54, 156; manufacture of, for Bavarian Army, 55–62

Coffeepot, improved, 159–61, 162

Cold: radiation of "frigorific rays," 156. See also Freezing

Combustion calorimeter, 72–74, 162

Committees of Safety, Rumford before, 14, 21

Concord, N.H., originally called "Rumford," 86; Rumford in, 9–15

Convection currents, 52–54, 109

Cooking, economics of, 72–76. See also Food; Stoves

Curwen, Judge Samuel, 29

Cuvier, Baron, 163–64

Dartmouth, Earl of, 24

Davy, Sir Humphry, 132–34, 162

Deux-Ponts, Duc de. See Maximilian Joseph, Elector of Bavaria

Dalton, John, 104

Double boiler, 75

Dynamometer, 156

Education of poor, 61–62

Einstein, Albert, 105–6

English Garden, 70–71, 84, 86, 115

Espionage: LaMotte case, 31–32; Rumford as spy in America, 13–22; Rumford as spy in Europe, 39–46

Faraday, Michael, 163

Farrington, Joseph, 130–31

Ferrous sulphate, 19

Fireless cooker, 75

Fireplaces, improvement of, 108–12

Food: economics of cooking, 72–76; gardens for, 69–71;

Food (cont'd)
  for poor, 60; Rumford
  soups, 65–67; water and
  nutrition, 63–65. See also
  Stoves
Freezing, 101–4, 142–43
French Academy of Sciences
  (French Institute), 138,
  144, 146, 147, 157, 163;
  lighted and heated by
  Rumford, 153–54, 161
"Frigorific rays," 156
Fuels, experiments with, 72–
  74

Gage, General Thomas, 17
Gallo-tannic acid, 19
Gardens, 69–71; English
  Garden, 70–71, 84, 86, 115
Garnett, Thomas, 130, 132
George III, King of England,
  37, 39; and Karl Theodor,
  119
George, Prince of Wales
  (George IV), 36
Germain, Lord George, 23–
  29
Gillray, James, 111, 112, 132
Gunpowder, experiments on,
  25–28

Hardy, Admiral, 26, 32
Harvard University: Rum-
  ford attends lectures at, 6;
  Rumford's bequest to, 163
Hay, Dr., 3–8
Heat: cold as separate from,
  156; from fuels, 72–74;
  Rumford's papers on, 80,
  92, 100, 161–62; thermal
  conductivity of cloth, 49–
  54. See also Caloric theory
  of heat; Radiation

Hippisley, Sir Coxe, 132
Holland, Elizabeth Lady,
  131–32
Holy Roman Empire, Rum-
  ford becomes Count of,
  85–86
Huntington, L.I., N.Y., Rumford in, 36

Invisible ink, 18–20
Ireland, Rumford in, 111
Italy, Rumford in, 86–87

Joule, James Prescott, 96–97

Karl Theodor, Elector of Bavaria, 38–40, 69–71; ap-
  points Rumford Minister
  to Great Britain, 118–19;
  calls Rumford back for
  war, 113–14; ennobles
  Rumford, 85–86; seeks
  apologies for Rumford, 84–
  85
Keith, Sir Robert, 38–39, 41
King, Rufus, 122–25
King's American Dragoons,
  Rumford as officer of, 33–
  37
Kitchen ranges, 74–75. See
  also Stoves
Kite experiment, 6–7

Lafayette, Marquis de, 163
LaMotte spy case, 31–32
Lamps, improved, 79–80,
  146–47, 153–54; lawsuit
  over, 147–50; portable,
  159, 162
Lavoisier de Rumford, Madame, courtship of, 138,
  141–44; married life, 145,
  150–52

Leslie (physicist), 110–11

Light, experiments in, 76–81, 153–54, 162; diffusing screens to improve illumination, 154

Liquids. See Water

London, England, Rumford in, 23–25, 29, 37, 39, 107–13, 121–39; assaulted by "highwaymen," 41, 107

McHenry, James, 123

Mannheim, Germany, 55–56, 114

Marion, General Francis, 36

Maximilian Joseph, Elector of Bavaria (Duc de Deux-Ponts), 38, 137–38

Medicine, Rumford's study of, 3–8

Military academy, U.S., 123–24

Military affairs. See Bavarian Army; British Army

Military Workhouse, 56–62, 64, 70, 75, 86

Moreau, General, 114–15

Munich, Germany: defended by Rumford, 114–16; English Garden in, 70–71, 84, 86, 115; honors Rumford, 86; Rumford's scheme for beggars of, 56–62; Town Council's opposition to Rumford, 84–85. See also Bavaria

Murray, Major David, 34

Napoleon I, Emperor of the French, 138, 141, 162

New Hampshire Militia, 21; Rumford as Major and informer in, 12–15

Nutgalls, 19

Nutrition. See Food

"Of Food," 66

"Of the Light Manifest in Combustion," 80

Order, Rumford's belief in power of, 164

Paris, France, Rumford in, 138, 143–63

Parquet, Jerome, 148

Passage thermometer, 49–52

Patents: lawsuit over, 147–50; Royal Institution and, 136–37

Perpetual-motion machine, 4–5

Photometer, 76–79

Physics not divorced from morals of society, 165–66

Piaggino (organizer of Institute), 57

Pictet, Professor, 130

Pig operation, 8

Pindar, Peter, 131

Poor People's Institute, 56–62, 64, 70

Porta, Jean Batista, 19

Potatoes, 65, 70

Pressure cooker, 75

"Propagation of Heat in Various Substances," 100

Prout, William, 54

Public-school system, 61–62

"Radiant caloric," 101

Radiation: fireplaces and, 108–12; of "frigorific rays," 156; Rumford's individually stoked steam radiator, 154–55. See also

Radiation (*cont'd*)
  Caloric theory of heat;
  Heat
Richardson, I., 4–5
Robins, Benjamin, 25–26
Rolfe, Benjamin, 9–10
Royal Institution of Great
  Britain, 127–39; Davy and,
  132–34, 162; financial
  problems of, 134–37; for-
  mation of, 127–32
Royal Society, 26, 113
Rumford, Count (Benjamin
  Thompson), life of. *See*
  Table of Contents
Rumford lamps. *See* Lamps
Rumford photometer, 76–79
Rumford Prizes, 112–13
Rumford soup, 66–67

Salem, Mass., Rumford in, 2
Sandwich, Lord, 32
Scientific insight must pre-
  cede technological devel-
  opment, 48, 63
Secret ink, 18–20
Signaling, naval, 28
Silk, experiments on, 30–31,
  51
Smoke reduction, 108–11
Soap, 161
Soups, 64–67
"Sources of Heat Which is
  Excited by Friction," 92
Spying. *See* Espionage
Steam engines, 136–37
Stoneland Lodge, 25–26
Stoves: cooking, 74–75, 111;
  portable field, 116–18
Strasbourg, Germany, Rum-
  ford in, 38

Talleyrand, Charles Maurice,

138
Talmadge, Benjamin, 36
Tay, B., 4
Temperature. *See* Caloric
  theory of Heat; Heat; Ra-
  diation
Thermal conductivity of
  cloth, 49–54, 156
Thermometer, passage, 49–
  52
Thilorier (lawyer), 149–50
Thompson, Benjamin (Count
  Rumford), life of. *See* Ta-
  ble of Contents
Thompson, David, 40
Thompson, James, 40
Thompson, Sarah Walker, 15,
  21; dies, 144; marries
  Rumford, 10
Thompson's Island, 40
Tyndall, John, *Heat as a
  Mode of Motion,* 96
Typhoid, 21

United States: Rumford's desire to return to, 121–25.
  See also American Revolution

Van de Graaff generator, 4
Vienna, Austria, Rumford in,
  39

Walker, Sarah. *See* Thomp-
  son, Sarah Walker
Walker, Reverend Timothy,
  9–10
War: Rumford defends Mu-
  nich, 113–15. *See also*
  American Revolution
Washington, George, 17
Water: freezing and contrac-
  tion of, 101–4, 142–43;

Water (*cont'd*)
   nutrition and, 63–65; mixing of, at temperature equilibrium, 104–6, 161
Watt, James, 136–37
Wentworth, Governor John, 10–15, 24
White Mountains survey proposed, 10–11
Williams, Reverend Samuel, 11
Wilmington, Mass., Rumford in, 8

Winthrop, Professor, 6
Woburn, Mass.: birth of Rumford in, 2; Rumford's apprenticeship in, 3–8; Rumford's return to, 17–21
Wolfeboro, N.H., 11
Wood, 162
Workhouses: in Ireland, 111; Military Workhouse, 56–62, 64, 70, 75, 86

Young, W., 4

SCIENCE STUDY SERIES

BATTAN, LOUIS J.   The Nature of Violent Storms, S 19
Radar Observes the Weather, S 24

BENADE, ARTHUR H.   Horns, Strings, and Harmony, S 11

BITTER, FRANCIS   Magnets: The Education of a Physicist, S 2

BONDI, HERMANN   The Universe at Large, S 14

BOYS, SIR CHARLES VERNON   Soap Bubbles and the Forces Which Mould Them, S 3

COHEN, I. BERNARD   The Birth of a New Physics, S 10

DAVIS, KENNETH S., and DAY, JOHN ARTHUR   Water: The Mirror of Science, S 18

DUBOS, RENÉ   Pasteur and Modern Science, S 15

FINK, DONALD G., and LUTYENS, DAVID M.   The Physics of Television, S 8

GALAMBOS, ROBERT   Nerves and Muscles, S 25

GAMOW, GEORGE   Gravity, S 22

GRIFFIN, DONALD R.   Echoes of Bats and Men, S 4

HOLDEN, ALAN, and SINGER, PHYLIS   Crystals and Crystal Growing, S 7

HUGHES, DONALD J.   The Neutron Story, S 1

HURLEY, PATRICK M.   How Old Is the Earth? S 5

JAFFE, BERNARD   Michelson and the Speed of Light, S 13

KOESTLER, ARTHUR   The Watershed: A Biography of Johannes Kepler, S 16

LITTAUER, RAPHAEL, and WILSON, ROBERT R.   Accelerators: Machines of Nuclear Physics, S 17

MAC DONALD, D. K. C.   Near Zero: The Physics of Low Temperature, S 20

OVENDEN, MICHAEL W.   Life in the Universe: A Scientific Discussion, S 23

PAGE, ROBERT MORRIS   The Origin of Radar, S 26

PIERCE, JOHN R.; DAVID, EDWARD E., JR.; and VAN BERGEIJK, WILLEM A.   Waves and the Ear, S 9

ROMER, ALFRED   The Restless Atom, S 12

SANDFORT, JOHN F.   Heat Engines, S 27

SHAPIRO, ASCHER H.   Shape and Flow: The Fluid Dynamics of Drag, S 21

SINGER, PHYLIS, and HOLDEN, ALAN   Crystals and Crystal Growing, S 7

VAN BERGEIJK, WILLEM A.; PIERCE, JOHN R.; and DAVID, EDWARD E., JR.   Waves and the Ear, S 9

WILSON, ROBERT R., and LITTAUER, RAPHAEL   Accelerators: Machines of Nuclear Physics, S 17